Disciplemaking With Guys

Jonathan Denton, Ph.D.

D6 FAMILY MINISTRY
114 BUSH RD · NASHVILLE, TN 37217 · 800.877.7030 · D6FAMILY.COM

Published by D6 Family Ministry

ISBN: 9781614841739

Contents

Part I
Crisis of Guys

The book of Nehemiah begins with a report that the city of Jerusalem was still in rubble 140 years after being destroyed by the Babylonians. Nehemiah wrote, "They said to me, 'The remnant in the province, who survived the exile, are in great trouble and disgrace. Jerusalem's wall has been broken down, and its gates have been burned" (Nehemiah 1:3). When Nehemiah heard the report, he wrote, "I sat down and wept. I mourned for a number of days, fasting and praying before the God of the heavens" (Nehemiah 1:4).

Nehemiah began his journey to rebuild the walls of Jerusalem by realizing the crisis, learning about the crisis, being honest with God about the crisis, and then seeking God for how to respond to the crisis. Disciplemaking with guys begins at this same point. As businessman and former presidential candidate Andrew Yang wrote in *The Washington Post*, "Here is one of the biggest problems facing America: Boys and men across all regions and ethnic groups have been failing, both absolutely and relatively, for years. This is catastrophic for our country."[1] This is a book that begins by looking at the current crisis of guys. My hope is that it will lead you to weep for our guys, like Nehemiah did for Jerusalem, but also to seek a vision from God for disciplemaking with guys.

Every adolescent guy needs to be surrounded by a team of caring, spiritually mature adults led (ideally) by his discipled parent(s). This team will disciple him on a well-defined path toward spiritual maturity utilizing male learning theory informed by Scripture. In this book, we'll look at these main ideas in four parts. As a starting point, the opening section, "Crisis of Guys," will look at the current crisis of boyhood. This section will begin with the hard work of disciplemaking with guys, dive into the details of how guys learn, and conclude with both the developmental needs of guys today and how our culture hurts guys.

As you read there will be plenty of examples where what I am suggesting applies to both guys and girls, but since this is a book about disciplemaking with guys, that's who I'll primarily be mentioning in the text. I also anticipate that some readers will be just beginning their journey in disciplemaking with guys. I have chosen to include some basics of disciplemaking that apply to both guys and girls to help every reader to feel equipped, while also applying these basic concepts specifically to guys.

The origin of my own love for disciplemaking with guys began in high school. I grew up in the Appalachian Mountains of East Tennessee. During the summer after my junior year, a summer intern at our church invited two others and me to meet with him to read *The Master Plan of Evangelism*. This was my first experience being in a discipleship group that met weekly, reading, studying, praying, and challenging one another. It was around this time that I learned about the call to take whatever I learn and teach it to someone else. I was challenged to step up in leadership positions and by my senior year in high school began to feel a call into ministry.

Later, while I was attending Clemson University, my former youth minister asked me if I would be interested in being a part-time youth director at a church near Clemson. I accepted the job and served there for three and half years. Nearing my graduation with a civil engineering degree, I wrestled with where God was calling me after graduation. I wasn't sure if God was calling me into a full-time career in engineering and to serve the church as a volunteer, serving bi-vocationally in ministry and engineering, or serving God full-time in ministry. My next steps became clear when at a campus ministry meeting a pastor read from 2 Corinthians 5:14, "For the love of Christ compels us" At that moment, I knew that God was speaking to me and that all I had done was because of the love of Christ in my life. As the passage continues in verse 15, "and he died for all so that those who live should no longer live for themselves, but for the one who died for them and was raised." I knew without a shadow of a doubt that God was calling me into full-time ministry, and I have sought to let Him direct each step of my path in this calling.

I moved to New Orleans for seminary and served in a variety of summer youth camp roles and interim youth ministry roles. As I did my doctorate in youth ministry, I also served full-time for ten years as associate pastor for students and discipleship at a church in Mississippi. During my twenty plus years of youth ministry to students, one of my greatest joys is getting to see students grow in their walks with God over time and go on to disciple their families and lead in ministry in both paid and volunteer roles.

I just finished my fifth year of teaching youth ministry at Charleston Southern University in Charleston, South Carolina. I am able to apply the concepts within this book to disciplemaking with collegiate guys, and I love training youth ministry guys and girls to do what I love: youth ministry! Along with teaching college students, I currently serve as a middle school small group leader in our church's middle school ministry where my wife is the middle school girls minister.

This book seeks to share what I have learned specifically about disciplemaking with guys. Disciplemaking involves three people: the *disciplemaker*, the *discipler*, and the *person who will be discipled.* Disciplemakers not only disciple, but train those they disciple to disciple others. I love where I am in life right now because I get to train the future disciplemakers of students and also get to disciple middle school guys as they begin the discipleship process. As I begin discipling guys in middle school, I am already preparing them to be future disciplemakers. I hope you will join me in this endeavor to be a disciplemaker of guys!

1

The Hard Work of Disciplemaking With Guys

One Sunday night I was running late for our high school guys discipleship Bible study. I was just starting my second year at a medium-size church in South Mississippi. My wife and I had launched discipleship Bible studies for guys and girls for the fall. Our discipleship groups for girls were thriving, but my group for guys was … surviving.

When I came into the room at the church that night, the guys were already there. They had found some playdough and made it into a baseball that they were using to play catch. I asked them to put it away so we could begin our Bible study. Trevor (names changed to protect identities) asked the infamous phrase that gets everyone into trouble: "Can we throw it one more time?" I told him no. The guys bargained. Cade had made a playdough target and the guys wanted to see if Trevor could hit it with their makeshift ball. I too wanted to see if he could hit it. "You can throw it one more time, but throw it easy," I unwisely said.

Meanwhile, the group of girls my wife was leading had grown so large that they split into two groups. The girls met at our house, with high school girls in our living room and a junior high group in our home office. The girls had set up a covenant with one another and were growing and sharing. My wife and the junior high leader usually ran out of time or went much later than the expected end time. The girls' group had so much to share and say—whereas my guys constantly asked me how long until we could go out to the field to play ultimate frisbee.

That Sunday night, I watched and waited to see if Trevor would hit the target. Instead of soft tossing it as I'd hoped, he scorched it like the last pitch in World Series game seven. Though he had the full confidence of a closer, he lacked the accuracy of a major league pitcher. The play dough ball went a full five feet to the left of the target and smashed through the second-floor window of the room where we were meeting. The playdough and shattered glass fell on a car in the parking lot. It was at this moment that I realized that I needed a new model for discipleship with these guys. After a full day of church activities, another "sit still while I instill" Bible study at the end of the weekend just was not working, but what had just happened didn't work either.

I knew that these guys were going to be future leaders of our ministry. Fast forward about six years and Trevor would be riding on the same plane as Mitt Romney on election night as one of his key interns. The guys in that group have grown up to become engineers, policy lobbyists, and doctors. And many are using their professions to the glory of God, like the one who runs a free medical clinic for those who cannot afford healthcare. Obviously, lots of other factors played in to where they are now vocationally, but the potential was always there. This is why disciplemaking matters so much. It is so easy to view our teenage guys as troublemakers and glass-breakers, or write them off as being disengaged or hopeless, rather see them as who they are: created by God with the potential to be used by Him both in their teenage years and throughout the rest of their lives.

After the playdough incident I began asking myself some questions. *I know these guys have been uniquely created by God with a purpose and design for their life. I also know that they are affected by sin that points them away from maturing in their Christlikeness. So how do I best disciple them? What ministry programs do we need to create or modify to best help them?*

Around the time that I began asking these questions, I began Ph.D. research into adolescent male learning theory. I began to read the works of authors such as Leonard Sax and Michael Gurian, who have led the way in recent years in researching the welfare of adolescent boys in the United States.

In today's world, boys are not doing well. In schools, boys receive more Ds and Fs than girls, comprise 80% of the discipline problems, and make up 70% of the children diagnosed with learning disabilities.[2] As adolescent boys graduate from high school, the issues are not resolved; many become magnified. Michael Kimmel, a sociologist who focuses on gender studies, labels the current collegiate landscape for males as "guyland." He defines guyland as a time when young men refuse to accept the responsibility of adulthood and remain in a lengthened state of adolescence. In guyland, young people attempt to prove their manhood by partying hard, staring at pornography, dating girls with little commitment to a relationship, hazing other male students, and having big dreams but no idea how to accomplish them.[3] This can then sometimes lead to drifting from major to major, job to job, and relationship to relationship.[4]

We have the great opportunity to disciple this generation of guys. This generation is hurting and in need of gospel-centered adults who will show the way. This generation also has incredible potential, potential that can be achieved when they are given a path to follow as they grow in their relationship with God. It's important to develop the skill of disciplemaking in the parents and leaders of the next generation of guys.

Intro to Disciplemaking

Through Jesus' example and teaching in the Gospels, we find a framework for disciplemaking a generation of guys. Jesus selected a group of guys that He would disciple while accomplishing our salvation through the cross and resurrection. The guys that Jesus chose were young as evidenced that only Peter and Jesus paid the temple tax (twenty years old or older).[5] He gives us the example of how to disciple young men into faith maturity and eventually ministry leaders who shaped the early church. Our guys today are hungry for this same pattern of discipleship.

Jesus discipled a small group of guys in a loving relationship, with gospel-centered teaching, and through experiential learning. Through this small group of guys, He impacted the whole world as they shared the gospel, discipled young believers, and launched the early church.

A look through the gospels reveals different aspects of discipleship that form a framework for the discipleship of guys. First, as Jesus states in Matthew 28:18–20:

> **All authority has been given to me in heaven and on earth. Go, therefore, and make disciples of all nations, baptizing them in the name of the Father and of the Son and of the Holy Spirit, teaching them to observe everything I have commanded you. And remember, I am with you always, to the end of the age.**

Jesus calls us as believers and leaders to make disciples of all nations. This call includes the next generation of adolescent guys. Leaders are to go with the authority of God and the presence of God. Teens are to be evangelized and discipled. They are to be taught the gospel and challenged to go and make other disciples. Teenagers are often taught this verse and challenged to go to the ends of the world to make disciples. We in youth ministry have understandably celebrated our teens' response to the gospel and to the Great Commission. If we stop there, however, we simply celebrate a head knowledge of discipleship, rather than the active disciplemaking we ought to pursue.

Although the Great Commission gives a rallying cry to disciplemaking, in the next book of the Bible Mark calls us to pause to reflect on the cost of discipleship. In Mark 8:34 Jesus states, "If anyone wants to follow after me, let him deny himself, take up his cross, and follow me." Even though we as youth leaders and parents are good at celebrating salvation, we often tend to minimize the cost of discipleship. This verse from Mark likely sounds foreign to an adolescent guy, who typically has had a smartphone since an early age, received participation trophies for athletics, and was given little to no boundaries on screentime and online gaming. Disciplemaking with adolescent guys is not only about helping them know things about God, but also challenging them to deny themselves and follow God wherever He leads. Teen guys should be encouraged to deny anything that takes the place of God in their hearts.

Continuing on through the New Testament, in the Gospel of John, we are challenged to "abide" in Christ (John 15). Jesus declares, "I am the vine; you are the branches. The one who remains in me and I in him produces much fruit, because you can do nothing without me" (John 15:5). Tim Keller defines an idol as "anything more important to you than God, anything that absorbs your heart and imagination more than God, anything you seek to give you what only God can give."[6] Guys today have lots of toys, games, dreams, relationships, and achievements that can absorb their hearts and imaginations. One of the primary roles of parents and youth leaders is helping guys recognize when anything begins to shape their identity or form purpose and meaning in their lives apart from God. We as disciplemakers are constantly calling guys back to abiding in Christ. Guys who are abiding in Christ display fruit in their lives.

As we mentor and encourage adolescent guys, we engage their heads through sharing the gospel and teaching them how to apply the gospel in their daily lives. We also challenge them to make disciples in their local community and throughout the world. We engage their hearts and encourage them to deny their idols and abide in Christ. And we engage their hands through helping them bear Godly fruit in every area of their life. This approach frames disciplemaking with guys.

Mapping Guys' Discipleship Journeys

When I was a youth minister, one of my favorite events was taking our graduating high school seniors on a ski trip. I absolutely loved taking students from the deep South (many of whom had never seen snow) to a steep slope and shoving them down the hill on two skis. The only thing funnier (and scarier!) was watching them try to go down a hill on a snowboard, especially if they caught the front edge. More importantly, though, the trip gave me an opportunity to celebrate these seniors and challenge them as they began to prepare for college. As much as I like to joke that I pushed them down the hill, in reality our ministry had a model we thoughtfully used to help unfamiliar students learn how to ski.

I grew up in East Tennessee and went skiing almost every year. As I took students who'd never done snow sports before on this trip, I had to develop a formula that would give them the best chance of success. First, I sent every new skier to ski school. In ski school, they would learn the basics of putting their skis on, skiing the pizza wedge, and getting on and off the ski lift. Ski school allowed me to hit the difficult slopes with my experienced skiers while our newbies were learning. After lunch on our first day, I would regroup the newbies and some of our more experienced adults to go out on the slopes together. Those of us who were experienced would give them personal training on how to read the ski map, how to ski under control, and most importantly, how to stop! Once our beginners learned to ski under control, their learning accelerated. We could ski alongside them, slowly allowing them to advance to more difficult slopes. With our guidance and plan, I even had a few beginner guys and girls become able to ski down some of the most difficult slopes with me on their first day!

This approach we used on our ski trip is a good roadmap for discipleship for guys. Many of our guys are sent out into their world with no training or support structure. They are strapped into their skis and pushed downhill. The carnage can be significant. The students on the trip who thought they could figure out skiing on their own without instruction ended up bruised and beaten, possibly injured. Sometimes they even injured someone else. Even though instruction is important in skiing, it is even more important in our walks with God. Many of our guys today are living out what it says at the end of Judges: "In those days there was no king in Israel; everyone did whatever seemed right to him" (Judges 21:25). They have been sent out into the world with no guidance or map. No wonder teens are often doing whatever seems right to them. What else are they to do?

Guys learning to walk with God need a group of discipled adults with a plan for their discipleship. Guys need leaders who will share the gospel with them and give them an on-ramp for discipleship.

As young believers, guys need a plan for their growth into spiritual maturity and a team of caring, spiritually mature adults who will walk alongside them on their discipleship journey. I like to spend regular time with new believers, going through the basics of the gospel and teaching them how to walk with God daily. Guys need a map that will take them on a journey from a new believer to a spiritually mature discipler ready to disciple others.

2

How Guys Learn

The fall of 2020 was a crazy time to be an assistant professor of Christian studies and student Ministry. I was in my third year teaching college students, but the world had changed. I was trying to navigate training youth ministers and teaching college students in a world that had drastically changed due to the COVID-19 pandemic. I spent many days standing in front of a classroom of college students all in masks while also teaching another group of students virtually through a livestream.

One day, I looked around and noticed that only females were in the classroom. In a class of forty, where were the guys on my roll? This wasn't just happening in one class, but in many classes in a row. Our college's usual attendance policies had been suspended because of the novelty of the pandemic. With the attendance policy gone, so were my guys. *The Wall Street Journal reported* in 2021 that the number of students enrolled at U.S. colleges and universities in 2020 had declined by 1.5 million compared to five years earlier. Seventy-one percent of the 1.5 million deficit were guys.[7] The world of education is wrestling with where guys have gone and how to teach guys effectively and engage them in the learning process. In student ministry, we also have moments when we ask, "Where are the guys at?" Learning theory, specifically male learning theory, gives some insight into where student ministry is with teaching males and how we can more effectively teach males.

Interactive Learning Theory

Before exploring male learning theory, L. S. Vygotsky's educational philosophy is worth examining. Vygotsky was a developmental psychologist who wrote about educational philosophy, among other things. His theory is helpful for student ministers because he examined the powerful relationship between a child and an adult in learning. Vygotsky proposed that the culture surrounding a child also impacts the child's mental development. Vygotsky contended that the learner creates meaning through social interaction. According to Vygotsky, humans do not learn solely through behaviorism as animals do, because they also learn through the knowledge of previous generations and through the knowledge constructed by their current collective social experience. Thus, Vygotsky concluded that human learning comes from a formula of reactions we inherit combined with historical, social, and individual experiences.[8] We must remember that as we teach and disciple guys there is a variety of contributors to the learning experience. The content of the lesson, along with the relationship of the leader and students, and the environment of the group contribute to discipleship.

To Vygotsky, it was not only the teacher and learner that are important in the learning process, but also the environment that the teacher creates, as well the relationship between all three.

When teaching Scripture to teenage guys, youth workers and teachers often think only about the content. We pick a Scripture passage, study it, and then give our guys the main points of the passage and a few applications. The guy, though, comes into the learning event with a story, with a history, with experiences, and with a wealth of knowledge, all while experiencing real-time interaction with the environment.

When we think about ministry to teen guys, we first need to consider our environment. Think through your teaching environment through the lens of a guy. Is the environment safe, encouraging, appropriately challenging, etc.?

Second, ask yourself what history the guys bring into your teaching event. I have begun to periodically lead my middle school guys' small group through a brain dump at the beginning of a new lesson. I ask them what they already know about the passage and what questions they may have about it. Once I know what the guys already know and what they want to learn, I can avoid boring students or stretching them too far by sharing content they are not prepared yet to learn.

Third, what is the guys' current experience with the topic? Some topics will easily hook their attention, while at other times we'll teach a biblical topic our guys have not had any direct experience with yet. If guys quickly answer your opening questions and get into easy discussion, then there is a good chance that they have thought about the subject or have been taught about it before. If they are quiet at the beginning, they may not have much confidence in their answers because it is a new idea or passage. In those instances, we must work harder to create what I call a "hook moment" (introduction that captures their attention) to show them the necessity of studying the topic. Sometimes, a guy may instantly shut down, like going quiet, because of a bad experience related to the content. When I recognize this (often with no warning), I may pause and ask if anyone would like to share their thoughts. If they do, I always thank them for sharing and then we begin to explore it. If no one shares, then I may approach the topic from a different angle or just tell them that they can always come talk to me afterward if they would like.

Vygotsky suggested that students learn most effectively when teaching is challenging but not too challenging, which he calls the "zone of proximal development." Vygotsky disagreed with evaluating a student through individual problem solving and suggested that evaluation should be in terms of what the student can solve in cooperation with a teacher.[9] A zone of proximal development exists between the actual developmental level of a guy and the potential development of that guy. Vygotsky defined the zone of proximal development as the difference between how far an individual could develop through independent learning and how far an individual could develop while learning under an adult mentor or peer mentors. And he claimed that teaching is most effective when it falls in this zone.[10] The teacher collaborates with the student so as not to teach above the potential development of the student, nor to teach below what the student has attained already through the actual development process. Discipleship opportunities allow youth workers great opportunities to know where a student is in their spiritual development and where they might want to go. This can be hard to do when students are in large groups, but easier in discipleship groups.

Parents are a great resource to help youth workers know where a student is, how a student best learns, and what their goals are. Some youth workers give formal times to meet with the parents of every teenager. I always let parents know that they could meet with me to discuss any concerns/questions they have about their guy. I also had lots of informal conversations with parents at church and in the community. Whenever I went to an event in which a student of mine was participating, I always sat with the student's parents to show them my support of the student and give me a large chunk of quality time with them. I would gain so much knowledge about where the student was, what he was struggling with, and where he could grow. With that knowledge, I could more accurately assess the next steps needed for a guy's discipleship.

It is impossible to determine the zone of proximal development for a room full of fifty to a hundred guys. One person simply cannot do that. However, if we have a team of caring adults then each one can be responsible for five to ten guys. Those adults can assess where an individual student is and where he can go.

Discipleship Groups: A Great Environment for Interactive Learning

When I was a junior in high school, our church hired a summer student ministry intern. Over the summer, that intern helped plan events for the student ministry, taught our summer Bible study, took us to play golf with him, and introduced us to World Cup Soccer. He also invited me and two other guys to meet weekly with him and read a book together. This was my first taste of discipleship, and it was life changing! We read the classic book by Robert Coleman, *The Master Plan of Evangelism*. This was the first time I sat with a group of guys to read a great book, talk about Jesus and how He discipled, challenge one another to grow deeper, and tell others about what we learned.

I longed for more of this in my life, and I experienced it through the college ministry that I was involved with at Clemson University, which was built on small groups and discipleship. My small group leader during my freshman year met every other week with me to go through our campus ministry's discipleship resources. As I began as a youth director at a local church, the senior pastor began meeting with me regularly to talk about ministry issues and my spiritual health. The director of our campus ministry at Clemson also discipled me through my junior and senior year of college. A lot of how I read the Bible, think about ministry, and practice spiritual disciplines was forged in these discipleship groups. As I began working in ministry, disciplemaking was one of my core values.

Discipleship in small groups like these is so effective because of the interactive learning that can take place. The discipler has been discipled and is a mature follower of Christ. The small size of the group provides a great opportunity for the discipler to decipher accurately where a guy's walk with God is and where the guy needs to be in his next step. A discipler also is able to assess a guy's understanding through their discussions together. This is hard to do in a large group.

Brain Development in Adolescence

Adolescent brain development also has important implications for teaching adolescent guys. As we better understand the process of brain development, we can gain knowledge of how best to help guys make decisions in this crucial stage and how we can make teaching and learning more effective for our guys.

When the brain develops, it goes through times of "blossoming and pruning." These periods of quick, intense growth (blossoming) overproduce connections. Life experiences then prune the excess connections back to only those used by the individual. The brain develops through the quick growth, and then strengthens used portions and connections and loses the non-used portions.[11]

Blossoming and pruning of the brain stop in childhood and then restart in adolescence. The prefrontal cortex is one area of the brain that experiences a significant amount of blossoming and pruning: the blossoming process peaks around eleven or twelve, but the pruning process does not create a mature prefrontal cortex until individuals are in their mid-twenties.[12] This is significant because the prefrontal cortex is the decision-making part of the brain that helps an individual plan, think through choices, and control impulses.

Though the prefrontal cortex is not yet developed in them, parents and adults should not believe that teenage guys need to be protected from having to make decisions. Instead, the exact opposite is true. Teenage guys need to make decisions because the process they go through to make those decisions is being "pruned" in their brains. If adults help adolescent guys make decisions wisely, then they will be more likely to make wise decisions in adulthood. This help is so important. Our guys are growing up in a world where all obstacles are being removed. We have transitioned from a "helicopter" stage, where adults hovered over the lives of guys and rescued them when they get in trouble, to a "lawnmower" stage, where adults mow down challenges before the kid even gets to them. As a youth worker, this might translate as parents calling to ask about the rooming list before an overnight event. Our guys need real opportunities to face real situations, think critically, and make decisions accordingly. In order to grow, they also need adults who will then help them look back thoughtfully on their decision making and critical thinking.

The window of opportunity is wide open for decision making and critical thinking during adolescence. In this influential period, connections both positive and negative are made and ingrained in teenage brains. At home and at church, adults can help shape a positive pathway in a guy's brain for learning and spiritual development. When wise, caring adults come alongside adolescent guys, we can help them practice positive decision making, deepening the brain patterns that lead to good outcomes.

What Can Happen When We Let Guys Try

When I was serving as a youth pastor, I had a high school guy ask me if I could help him with a concert he was putting together. I said "Sure, who is playing?" He then listed two well-known Christian worship bands. He had reached out to the bands and found a way to book them to our little town in Mississippi. I couldn't believe it. My first reaction was to tell him all the ways this could go wrong or say that it was too big of a project for him to undertake. I could have told him I didn't want to get wrapped up in doing all of the work that would undoubtedly come with an event of this scale.

Instead, I decided to listen to him—probably because I was so shocked he had pulled this much off that I didn't know what else to say. Within the next few weeks, he secured two sponsors to pay for the whole event and sold the minimum number of tickets to guarantee the tour stop. I could not have done this myself. This high schooler also organized all of his friends and many adult volunteers for the event. My one piece of advice to him was to make sure the bands knew he was seventeen before they showed up!

Of course, there were things that he could have done better and things we helped him out with. However, I learned through this experience the incredible things that teenage guys can do if we give them the chance, offering guidance along the way. Although this is a pretty unique story and not one that I would recommend challenging your guys to imitate, all of our guys face moments every day that provide them opportunities to grow in their decision making and critical thinking. Our call is to encourage them and guide them to be used by God in their unique situations.

Brain Differences Between Males and Females

One innovation that is advancing our understanding of male learning is brain imaging. Through brain imaging, scientists have studied the differences between the male and female brain. Though men and women are more similar than different in their brain structures, studies have found at least one hundred differences between male and female brains.[13] Although there isn't total consensus, many scientists agree on the major differences in the male and female brain and the brain's development in adolescence.

The male brain is structurally different from the female brain. The corpus callosum is a bundle of tissues containing approximately 200 million myelinated fibers that connect the right and left hemispheres of the brain. The effects of gender differences on the corpus callosum have been debated, with some researchers finding a significant difference in the size of a boy's corpus callosum compared to that of a girl, while many others find no significant differences.[14] Studies of young people at various ages have found different patterns of growth or different rates of growth across the genders, which may account for some of the differences in the findings.[15] Whether or not a difference of size exists, it's generally agreed upon that more crosstalk exists between the hemispheres in the female corpus callosum than the male corpus callosum. With more crosstalk, girls have a greater ability to multitask than guys.[16]

The frontal lobe (the decision-making part) of the female brain tends to be more active and grow at earlier ages than the frontal lobe of the male brain. This may account for why we see adolescent males as more impulsive than adolescent females. The Broca's and Wernicke's areas—main language centers of the brain—are also located in the frontal and temporal lobes. In the female brain, these areas develop earlier and are more advanced when compared to male brains at similar ages. With these developed areas, females tend to have more neural pathways for word production and have a great volume of words for experience and emotion.[17]

Between males and females not only are there structural differences in the brain, but differences in hormone levels and blood flow. Boys tend to have more dopamine—associated with increased impulsive behavior—in their bloodstream. The cerebellum—the part of the brain most involved in doing—tends to receive more blood flow in guys' brains than in girls. Whereas girls have higher levels of estrogen and oxytocin, boys tend to have higher levels of testosterone and vasopressin. With the higher levels of oxytocin, females tend to learn better through verbal communication. With the higher levels of vasopressin, males tend to learn better through active learning.[18]

Finally, a guy's brain takes rests in order to recharge, whereas a girl's brain is still active during rest.[19] If, for instance, a guy is squirming or fidgeting in a small group, he is actually just keeping his brain awake.

Brain Research on Male Learning

With a differently structured brain, teenage guys learn differently than teenage girls in a few ways. First, the male brain is designed primarily for spatial activity rather than for emotional relationships. Guys have the neuron capacity for processing emotions, but their brain is not as strongly structured for emotive skills as the female brain. While girls have historically needed a brain structured with emotive skills, guys have historically needed a brain designed for spatial skills like hunting and building.[20] Guys' brains have historically been used for active learning in their environment.

Second, the male brain tends to focus the adolescent male outward into his world rather than inward to his own emotional development.[21] One of the driving forces behind the push into the world is what Gurian and Stevens refer to as "boy energy." Boys have a natural drive that becomes a powerful force in adolescence.[22] This energy comes with a great potential for innovation and also tends to drive males toward purpose and meaning.[23]

Third, the male brain often utilizes deductive reasoning to reason abstractly: boys tend to start with generalizations and then move on to the specific. Girls tend to use inductive reasoning by starting with the concrete and then building generalizations. Girls also tend to trust their intuitions, while guys tend toward a preference to trust things that are backed up with logic they can understand.[24] While teaching guys the Bible, I spend a significant amount of time discussing the details of the text, but I also want to stretch them to think about the implications of the text for their life and relationships. I also try to seek ways to engage their heart and worship toward God as a response to the text.

Ministry Implications From Male Learning Theory

One of my favorite classes to teach in college is Student Ministry Internship. The primary component of the class is the student's internship in a local church's student ministry. I love having collegiate women in the course and hearing about their experiences. I also love having guys in the internship course. Their level of engagement in this course is different from other courses because the course is designed in the way that many guys learn best. They are actively serving in the field and spend most of the time talking about what they are experiencing. The books they read through that class are tied closely to what they are doing. They also meet weekly with a ministry mentor where they talk about their coursework and their ministry experience. For guys, the experiential components in this course provide an ideal context for some of their best learning.

Because boys and girls learn differently in many ways, we must rethink disciplemaking with guys. First, we must motivate our guys into the lessons in our small groups. Guys are not designed to sit still for long periods of time with lots of words being thrown at them. This does not mean that we can't teach for extended periods, as evidenced by students who will binge watch shows, watch hour long online tutorials for their favorite games, or listen to whole seasons of podcasts. When guys are prepared for what they are doing and it is a topic that they have a desire to learn about, they can invest long periods of time in that subject. If not, they can quickly become disconnected from the lesson we are teaching. One of the best ways to engage guys is to be genuinely excited about the topic we are teaching. When I am passionate about the lesson, my guys often want to know why.

Second, guys tend to learn best through active engagement. Disciplemaking with guys is an opportunity to actively engage them in the learning of God's Word. Active learning techniques can be helpful in both large group and small group settings. I share some techniques I like to use later in the book.

Third, discipleship must involve real-world applications. Student ministries must make sure that guys are encouraged and driven to live their faith out in the world. We want to give guys ideas for application in individual lessons, and then follow up by actually asking how that application went. We also want to find ways to engage guys in service and leadership opportunities in the church and in missions locally and globally.

3

Developmental Needs of Guys

In 2004, I started my first semester of seminary. The move from little ol' Clemson to the Big Easy, New Orleans, was a major one. I loved New Orleans, but after I'd spent several months there, I was really excited about going back to Clemson for spring break. One of the reasons was that I was going to go on the first date with my good friend, who is now my wife. I was also excited to see my friends who were seniors about to finish college. They were excited to see me as well and wanted to show off their latest ideas. We had led together in our collegiate ministry and were always coming up with creative ideas for our ministry's big events. This year, they were going to Daytona for a spring break collegiate ministry week. My friends were planning the nightly program. Each night they planned to hold worship for several collegiate groups.

My friends had the grand idea that they wanted confetti to blast out when the emcee walked onto stage for the opening night, and they were testing how to make it happen when I visited. They first tried a leaf blower filled with confetti but that did not work. Many of them were engineering majors, so they decided to build a confetti canon (this was before you could just buy anything you needed on Amazon). They somehow built this confetti cannon out of a CO2 tank and PVC pipe. Please do NOT try this at home!

When I arrived to see them at Clemson, they were so excited to show me what they had built. They filled the canon with CO2, turned the dial, and … barely two pieces of confetti flew out. We all know that guys do not like to be shown up by technology. They regrouped. Without me knowing it, one of my friends decided to max out the pressure. And then, KABOOM! The pipe burst. In the spring heat of the South, it began to snow white PVC pieces. One hit me hard enough that I instantly fell to the ground. One of my friends ran to me, gathered me in his arms, and yelled out, "I love you, man!" because he thought I was gone and had never told me he loved me. The friend who owned the house ran in from the back room and saw the scene: PVC snow all over the yard, and me cradled in our other friend's arms. His response? "Did y'all get that on video?!?"

Guys have incredible potential for ingenuity and creativity. This statement is not intended to diminish the great growth we have seen in opportunities for girls and all the work that we need to do in terms of encouraging and supporting women in STEM fields. I absolutely love having collegiate females in my courses and encourage them to follow God into whatever field He calls them to. I love celebrating their success! At the same time, God has uniquely created guys to learn and grow in the ways detailed in the previous chapter. For the confetti canon, it was a thin line between having enough pressure to propel the confetti out of the canon and adding so much pressure that there was an explosion. As we minister to guys, we encounter the thin line between pushing guys deeper in their walk with God and driving them away, especially with the current pressures guys face on a daily basis. In this chapter, I want to discuss four factors that are putting pressure on the natural development of guys. We want to acknowledge these so that we understand the context in which we are ministering to our guys. We will then look in the rest of the book on how to help them grow in this context through disciplemaking.

Four Challenges Straining Developmental Needs of Guys

In college, I was employed by a construction company as a civil engineering co-op student, working on projects where our company was building water treatment plants. Part of my job was to help the professional engineers read the drawings of the completed projects and plan the work. We created project timelines by determining which steps needed to be completed and in which order. All the steps in the project timeline built upon one another. If a step was missed or delayed, all the future steps were affected.

Teenage guys are not finished products. They are in the developmental stage moving from childhood to adulthood. Through this time, they have a set of needs. When this natural stage of development is delayed or hindered, all the future developmental stages are affected. There are four challenges that can disrupt this developmental stage for guys today: changes in education, loss of family members and other men, failure to launch into manhood, and lagging faith maturity.

Challenge #1: Changes in Education

The way we in the Western world currently teach guys is not helping teenage them in their development. Leonard Sax, a physician, Ph.D. psychologist, and author on the current challenges that boys and girls face, notes that one change that has hurt boys is the movement from *Kenntnis* to *Wissenchaft*. *Kenntnis* is a German word that means "to know by experience" and refers to the knowledge generated from experiences with the world. *Wissenchaft* is a German word that means "to know something" and refers to the knowledge gained from books. "For boys in particular, emphasizing *Wissenchaft* while ignoring *Kenntnis* may seriously impair development—not cognitive development but the development of a lively and passionate curiosity,"[25] Sax writes. Today's boys no longer learn through apprenticeships or as they hunt in clans outdoors, but rather through books and lectures in the classroom. The longer boys have to sit still and listen, the more their brains are taxed. This is not anything against books—books are great for boys! I love listening to what my son is learning through the books he reads. The problem is when *Wissenchaft* is the only type of learning that guys experience.

This focus on knowledge-gathering is also evident in the church. Though churches do this in various forms—some with a master teacher format of large group teaching and then discussion or a more traditional structure of a Bible lesson in small groups—there is still a large, long section of time where guys are asked to sit still while a leader teaches. If you look around the room of guys during the teaching time—and even in the discussion time—what do you see? Typically, there are a couple of guys who are highly engaged, a few who are totally disengaged, and the rest who at any moment are listening, zoning off, distracting others, or being distracted. Something is not working!

Do not hear me wrong: Guys need to learn to sit, listen, and engage deeply with whatever subject we are teaching, including the Bible! However, we teachers may not be using the best methods to help our guys learn. Our primary mode of teaching has shifted to lecture with some large group discussion questions. A teacher studies the Word of God and prepares a sermon or lesson. That teacher then lectures for thirty minutes while guys are asked to sit still. Then questions are asked of those guys and in response we have … silence. We are emphasizing *Wissenchaft* while ignoring *Kenntnis*. As we saw in the previous chapter, guys' brains are being taxed with lots of word intake and little experience.

Bible scholars commonly refer to Luke chapters 9–13 as the "travel narrative." During these ten chapters, Jesus walked with His disciples from Galilee to Jerusalem, teaching them through parables. Jesus taught through both by *Wissenchaft* and *Kenntnis*. At times, Jesus sat down with His disciples and taught them, like in the Sermon on the Mount. At other times, He walked and taught through practical experiences along the way. In what ways are we teaching through experience to our guys?

Challenge #2: Loss of Family Members and Other Men

Another current challenge to boys is the lack of family members and other men in their lives outside the immediate home. All past cultures have asked the immediate and extended family to train and teach young kids. Today, boys learn from classroom teachers who are largely disconnected from the rest of the guy's life, versus learning from a family-led education team. I saw a meme the other day that said, "They say it takes a village to raise a child. Where is this village and is there a number to call?"

The presence of men is important in the development of an adolescent guy. As Warren Farrell and John Gray write in their book *The Boy Crisis*,

> I discuss men in a book about boys because men are the role models who either offer your son structure and inspiration, or leave him rudderless and depressed. Especially with his dad, the boy tends to become what he sees in the men around him: 'like father, like son,' 'he's a chip off the old block.' Or they are the role models who leave your son scared as to how to pursue life.... If he cannot articulate what scares him, he may withdraw into video games and video porn and develop a virtual life to mask his depression. What is past is prologue.[26]

Throughout the Old Testament, we see that one generation is tasked with telling the next about the work of God. As Joel proclaims, "Tell your children about it, and let your children tell their children, and their children the next generation" (Joel 1:3). Some generations of men in the Old Testament did this well, while other generations failed.

The presence of a father is especially crucial in the life of a guy. Farrell writes,

> Dads—like moms, air, and water—are essential to our lives. But we've tried to live without dads. We haven't tried to live without moms, air, or water. Why is it that in a generation pro-

> ducing some outstanding young men, whether a boy is in crisis or leading us out of a crisis is signifiantly influenced by whether he is dad-deprived or dad-enriched? Dad-enriched boys tend to fill the purpose void with constructive new senses of purpose; dad-deprived boys are more likely to either drown in their purpose void, or fill it with destructive senses of purpose.[27]

A great example of a dad who enriches his family is Joshua, who says, "As for me and my family, we will worship the LORD" (Joshua 24:15).

Challenge #3: Failure to Launch Into Manhood

A third challenge to guys today is that they are failing to launch into mature manhood and have little motivation to do so. In his research on adolescent males between sixteen and twenty-six, Michael Kimmel writes, "Today's young men are coming of age in an era with no road maps, no blueprints, and no primers to tell them what a man is or how to become one."[28] An important role of the family and church is to provide a picture of a mature, Christ-following man and a blueprint for how to develop into that type of man. Yet, many of our guys are wandering through life without purpose, meaning, or mission.

One of the primary tasks of the church is helping the next generation launch into spiritual maturity with a proper road map. Asaph states in Psalm 78,

> He established a testimony in Jacob and set up a law in Israel, which he commanded our ancestors to teach to their children so that a future generation—children yet to be born—might know. They were to rise and tell their children so that they might put their confidence in God and not forget God's works, but keep his commands (Psalm 78:5–7).

As I wrote earlier, every generation has a responsibility to teach the next generation about God and His works so that the new generation follows and obeys God. This mandate also specifically applies to men regarding the next generation of guys. Paul instructs older men in Titus 2,

In the same way, encourage the young men to be self-controlled in everything. Make yourself an example of good works with integrity and dignity in your teaching. Your message is to be sound beyond reproach, so that any opponent will be ashamed, because he doesn't have anything bad to say about us (Titus 2:6–8).

A few years ago, my family decided to start a vegetable garden. As we began planning the garden, it took me back to riding with my granddad to his garden. We would jump in his old Ford truck and drive to the garden. Instead of turning on the air conditioning, he'd just tell me to crack the window (not even the main window, but a little triangle window in the corner). We would then drive up and down the rows as he taught me how to tend to each type of plant. Almost thirty years later, all of those memories and lessons came rushing back as I started a garden with my own family. Before I planted my garden, I went to a retired guy in our church who I knew grew a great garden each summer. He invited me to his house and showed me all the different ways he plants and how he tends to them. After I planted my garden, he even came over and gave me tips. I still use those same tips today. Generations of men helped shape my own family's garden.

This is a great example of what our guys need today. Our guys need family members, extended family, and other adults and men in their lives. Our guys need a variety of people they can go to for information. Just as my granddad and my retired friend gave me a plan to build a garden, our guys need others who will help them map out their mission and purpose. They need an extended network of adults who will show them a picture of who they should be and how to get there.

Challenge #4: Lagging Faith Maturity

A final challenge inhibiting guys' development is their lagging faith maturity. Faith maturity is the development of their understanding about God, the transformation of their life through their walk with God, their connection with a church family, and their practice of faith that models the belief of their church.[29] Teenagers are in a unique stage where they are not only growing in their personal relationship with God (what we typically think about in discipleship) but also through a series of typical developmental changes in how they understand and think about faith. James W. Fowler, a minister and a professor in the field of human development, wrote about the development of faith through the lifetime of a child. He described teenagers as developing new mental abilities in adolescence that make spiritual development possible. During adolescence, they then begin to personalize their beliefs and form their religious identity alongside their peers.[30] A personal religious identity is a new development that occurs during adolescence. And God has designed for adolescents to go through this development in this period of their lives.

Adolescents begin to reflect on life experiences and develop meaning and purpose from those experiences. With the new cognitive abilities, adolescents can think about abstract ideas. Teens can reflect on their faith and the faith of their parents. Adolescent males are developmentally ready for adults to lead them toward Christ for their life meaning and purpose, and for the fulfillment of their relational needs.

Researcher and professor Christian Smith found in a national study on youth and religion that student faith is divided more or less equally between students who believe that faith is an important matter and students who believe that faith is not particularly important. Smith concluded that adolescents are divided fairly evenly into three groups. "One third of U.S. teens experience an intimate relationship with God, another third feel something in the middle, neither intimate nor distant, and almost one third of U.S. teens either feel distant from or do not believe in God."[31]

Smith's national study on youth and religion also found that teen faith preference is similar to parental faith preference. The study found that about 75% of adolescents "consider their own religious beliefs somewhat or very similar to their parents." In contrast, few consider their religious beliefs very different from those of their mother (6%) or father (11%).[32] Teens typically exhibit the same preference of religious faith as their parents. As Smith summarized for parents, "We'll get what we are."[33]

A research study of effective Christian education by Search Institute concluded that the two strongest influences on the faith maturity of adolescents are family religiousness across the lifetime of an adolescent and the Christian education involvement across the lifetime of an adolescent.[34] An adolescent guy needs both the family and the church as he develops into a mature Christ follower.

There is a significant difference between genders in the religiosity of adolescents. In the national study on youth and religion, teenage girls scored significantly higher in all six religiosity measures than teenage boys: religious service attendance, importance of religious faith shaping daily life, personal commitment to live life for God, current involvement in a religious youth group, frequency of teen praying alone, and closeness the teen feels to God.[35] Many youth workers would agree with this research finding because they see it each week in their ministry. Teenage guys are lagging in faith development.

A couple of weeks ago, we celebrated our eighth-grade students before they headed to senior high ministry. We had the eighth-grade girls come onto stage and share one thing that they enjoyed and one thing they had learned during their time in middle school ministry. We then gave the eighth-grade guys the same opportunity. As you can imagine, the girls spoke longer than the guys, but I was impressed with what my guys said. I had been one of their small group leaders since sixth grade. Almost all of them mentioned small group as their favorite thing of the middle school ministry, and many shared great things they had learned. Their words reminded me of the power of adults who are consistent in guys' lives, small groups where guys can gather weekly to encourage one another, and the Word of God that can take root in their lives when it's read consistently.

Part II

Rebuilding From Crisis to Disciplemaking

Nehemiah longed to rebuild the walls of Jerusalem. When King Artaxerxes asked Nehemiah why he was sad and what he requested, Nehemiah prayed to God and then responded to the king this way: "If it pleases the king, and if your servant has found favor with you, send me to Judah and to the city where my ancestors are buried, so that I may rebuild it" (Nehemiah 2:5). When the king sent Nehemiah to rebuild, Nehemiah began his preparations for the work with a team of men. " I got up at night and took a few men with me. I didn't tell anyone what my God had laid on my heart to do for Jerusalem.... I inspected the walls of Jerusalem that had been broken down and its gates that had been destroyed by fire" (Nehemiah 2:12–13). After Nehemiah saw the work to be done, he called out to the people, "You see the trouble we are in. Jerusalem lies in ruins and its gates have been burned. Come, let's rebuild Jerusalem's wall, so that we will no longer be a disgrace" (Nehemiah 2:17).

The first part of the book showed some of the challenges facing guys in our ministries. It is easy to respond with tears over our guys like Nehemiah did when he heard about the broken walls. As ministers, we have all felt the pain that Nehemiah felt. We have woken up thinking about our students. We have shared our frustrations with other youth workers. We have also prayed intensely for our guys. We can learn from Nehemiah, who saw the reality of the moment and also called the Israelites to begin to rebuild the walls. In Part II, we will learn to follow Nehemiah's example as we prepare to rebuild from crisis to disciplemaking.

4

A Clan of Relationships

In the Intro to Student Ministry collegiate class I teach, I have my students write out the names of adults who have had a significant spiritual impact in their life. Within a minute, most students will have written between five and eight names. I then have them share with others in the class why they wrote who they did. I always wish those adults could hear what the students share! I truly believe one of the main reasons these students are sitting in a ministry class at a Christian college is because of the investment of these adults in the lives of these students.

I challenge you to pause and think about the names of adults who had a significant spiritual impact in your life when you were a kid or teenager. Write their names in the margin here, or on a sheet of paper. Some of you might write one or two names and some might write ten or more. Look at your list and think about the different types of adults who influenced your life spiritually. My list includes my parents, a husband and wife teaching team who taught first graders in our church for over fifty years, a female youth worker who stayed committed to God's call through a crisis, men who taught my small groups as volunteers, pastors who took time to mentor me, college leaders who discipled me, and professors who equipped me both inside and outside of the classroom. I would not be where I am today without this team of caring adults. Our guys today need teams like this as well.

The previous chapter spoke about four challenges that are straining the developmental needs of guys. This chapter will speak about what guys need in their lives to meet these needs: a clan of relationships, three faith families, and a team of spiritually mature men.

A Clan of Relationships

One of the missing pieces in the lives of teens today is a variety of relationships. Students need not only their immediate family but also a team of caring adults. Teens are more prone to grow in their faith when they are surrounded by multiple adults who are living out their faith. A clan of relationships is important in every culture. As Leonard Sax writes, "There is no enduring culture in which parents attempt this task alone. As the saying goes, it takes a village to raise a boy to manhood or a girl to womanhood."[36]

Michael Gurian claimed that three families are needed to raise an adolescent guy to mature manhood. The first family is the teenage guy's immediate family, usually including parents and grandparents. The second family is his extended family, which includes blood relatives, friends, teachers, and mentors. The third family is the guy's community family, which includes cultural influences like media and youth culture, church groups, and community groups and leaders.[37] To transition into manhood, teenage guys need a team of caring adults in their home, church, and community.

As youth workers, we see teens struggling because of problems in all three of these areas. When the immediate family is unhealthy or in crisis, a teenager may struggle in all other areas of his or her life. Today, teens may experience any or all of these: divorce, single parenting, fatherlessness, abuse, death of a parent, major conflict, blended families, isolation/distance from close relatives, grandparents as primary caretakers, and homelessness. Thus, the extended family and the community family are sometimes called upon to take on the role of the immediate family. One major complaint of youth workers is about the lack of parental guidance in guys' lives, and it's valid: When the student does not have a strong immediate family, the extended family and community family have the privilege of undertaking a much harder job.

I had a wake-up call when I asked a new student for his home address while registering him for youth group. He couldn't give me a stable address because he was moving from house to house every few weeks. When we encounter a teen like this or one who is going through a crisis in the home, we should approach the situation with the kind of care we'd show someone in the ICU. They might need immediate assistance. The answer for the student could be a place to stay, counseling/care sessions with the pastoral team or a licensed therapist, a grief support group, or financial help. Our churches can also be a help to our community when our adult ministries and family ministries are supporting and discipling healthy families for our students. Healthy families are then in the community impacting other families through things like modeling a healthy family, having helpful conversations with other families, connecting families to resources that they may need, and fostering kids while parents seek help.

Teens are also stronger when they have a strong extended family. Teachers, coaches, trainers, directors, mentors, and extended family relatives help encourage teens in all areas of their lives. Many members of the "second family," as we can think of this network of people, spend a lot of time training, molding, and shaping a teenager. It's wise for us as youth workers to find ways to support and disciple these important adults in a student's life. Many guys have been discipled by their coaches, both for good and for bad. We should encourage parents to be thoughtful when considering which adults they allow to care for and instruct their student. As a youth worker or small group leader, we often are part of a student's second family. God also gives us opportunities to disciple and counsel some of our guys in more specific/intensive ways than others. Often, these relationships become some of our favorite moments of ministry.

One task for youth workers is to challenge parents to think about healthy second environments for their children. Many parents today find activities that interest their children. Our oldest son took an interest in tennis and wanted to get better, so we signed him up for a tennis team. It is easy as a parent to just think about the specialized training that they will get in their activities. One of the things we can do as student ministers is to challenge parents to think about the environment. Is it a caring environment for the child? Will it help the child grow in his or her faith or at least not distract them away from their faith? Simply making these questions a part of the conversation in choosing activities is a first step for many parents. It is easy as a parent of a guy to only consider if the training is helping them in skill development, but there is a lot more we can take into account. Guys need healthy second environments that can help them grow in the unique talents God has given them. Because these areas shape guys in incredible ways, let's make sure that these second environments are healthy environments that build character and skill and do not become the only world where guys live.

We also want to have our communities of faith play a large role in our students' third family—the community family. Sometimes, youth ministry is attacked for trying to be a first family. Some even believe that youth ministry should not exist because they think it hurts the first family's ability to serve as primary disciplemakers. The problem comes about not simply because of the existence of youth ministries, but when youth ministries try to usurp the first family's role. A teenager needs both an immediate family and a community of faith. A youth ministry helps grow the third family when it's a place where students gather with peers and are discipled by spiritually mature adults. When functioning as a healthy third family, a youth ministry will also find ways to connect teens with the larger faith family. Chap Clark, one of the great thinkers in youth ministry, contends that one of the most frequent images of the church in the Bible is the term "family." Students are not just participants in our ministries, they are adopted into the family of God. Thus, we should think about ministry in terms of ministry to students who are not disconnected from the rest of the church, but rather are "brothers and sisters" with the rest of the church. He states,

> The goal of youth ministry as adoption is for every child, every adolescent, and every young adult to be so embraced by the community of faith that they know they always have a home, a people, and a place where they can discover who they are and how they are able to contribute. In short, youth ministry is adopting young people into the family of God.[38]

Three Relationship Clans and Faith

The specifics of the three clans of relationship in a teen's life are strong predictors of a student who prioritizes and practices a vibrant and life-transforming faith. A study found a large correlation between the number of caring environments teens were part of (home, school, and church) and the adolescent's faith maturity. In this case, a caring environment meant an environment that showed love, care, and warmth. This study found that only 5% of adolescents who had no caring environments had a mature faith. Only 17% of adolescents with one caring environment scored a mature faith. In comparison, 30% of adolescents who were part of two caring environments exhibited a mature faith, and 53% of adolescents who had three caring environments exhibited a mature faith.[39]

Michael Gurian suggests that "a parent-led team" should surround every teenage guy. The parent-led team includes a variety of adults who support the education and growth of the adolescent male.[40] The team begins with the parents, who reach out to other family members and adults in the community who can help educate the boy.

I really like this concept of a parent-led team and think it has huge implications for disciplemaking with guys. Adolescents need a variety of adults to disciple them. This team of caring adults will ideally be designed and led primarily by the student's parent. Thus, the parent is still the primary disciplemaker in the life of a guy but is partnering alongside the church and other spiritually mature adults for care and discipleship.

A clan of committed, caring adults is also important in ministry to students. Richard Ross writes that "students who have heart connections with at least five significant, spiritually alive adults have the best opportunity to develop a sustainable, alive faith embracing the supremacy of Christ."[41] We often talk about the need to have one adult for every five students on a youth trip or in a youth program. When it comes to discipleship, we need to flip the script and have five adults for every one student. That does not mean that we need to have five adults involved for every student in every program. We do, however, want to provide opportunities for every student to connect with multiple different adults throughout their time in our ministry. Our goal should be that every student who is involved, from junior high to senior high, will graduate with five significant relationships with adults.

Ron Hunter, executive director and CEO of D6 Family Ministry and cofounder and director of the D6 Conference, contends that "generational discipleship" is needed in the church. Generational discipleship comes about when the church and the home work together strategically. The model comes from Deuteronomy chapter 6. Hunter writes, "In Deuteronomy 6, God commands the older generation of grandparents, parents, and the faith community as a whole to exercise generational discipleship by example and diligent instruction, and not to delegate this role to anyone else."[42] Discipleship of the next generation takes the whole church family. We join hands together to model a vibrant faith, guide students to the beauty of the gospel, and shape their hearts for a lifetime of faith.

Deuteronomy 6 contains the verses known as the Shema: "Listen, Israel: The Lord our God, the Lord is one. Love the Lord your God with all your heart, with all your soul, and with all your strength" (Deuteronomy 6:4–5). These words express the essence of being an Israelite and faithful follower of God. And how were the Israelites to know this instruction? Through the family and faith community passing these teachings on to their children. They were to be written "on the doorposts of your house and on your city gates" (Deuteronomy 6:9). Thus, at that time a child would learn in the rituals of the home and throughout the faith community. We can learn from all of this as we consider how the three families can work in tandem in order for a child to grow and practice a vibrant, life-transforming faith.

Role of Men in Motivating Teenage Guys

Adolescent guys also need additional men in their lives. Men teach adolescent males a variety of things about manhood. First, men teach teenage guys how to behave in the world.[43] Second, men teach male identity to teenage guys. As Gurian writes, "The greatest gift [men] give [to boys] is the *male identity*.... This identity is not passed on in a sentence or a phrase—it is passed on through years of male involvement with male children."[44] Connections with other men create pathways for the teachings of manhood.

When I think back to how I gained an understanding of manhood, it came both through teaching and modeling. It should not come from cultural ideas, but through Scripture and the example of Jesus. Many of these concepts are conveyed and honed within the church. Within individual churches, one worthy exercise is to gather a group of mature adult men together to study Scripture in order to set the vision for developing a biblical definition of manhood for our guys.

In addition to learning from manhood within the church, I also learned by observing individuals. I would watch the way my dad would handle situations, lead our family, and serve in our church. There is a reason we say, "Like father, like son." The son imitates his father. I also paid attention to my mentors, noticing how they lived gospel-centered lives. When I began serving in a church, I imitated the mentors of mine who served in youth ministry. When I began teaching, I imitated my professors. Adolescent guys need spiritually mature men in their lives to observe and imitate.

Guys also benefit from female mentors. My youth minister was a woman, and I would not be where I am today without her example of trusting God in a difficult time in her life and ministry, modeling to me the characteristics of a faithful youth worker, and training me in youth ministry while I was her intern. I am where I am now because of the variety of adults who poured into my life, especially her. Find male leaders to mentor young guys in small group settings, discipleship settings, and ministry settings, and also invite female leaders as well to connect with guys, set an example of following God, and encourage them in their walks with God.

Who's on the Dock?

There's a scene I love that takes place at the conclusion of Marvel Studios' *Avengers: Endgame*. The Avengers are at the river paying remembrances to Tony Stark. The camera pans down the dock and then up to the cabin, showing the faces of the people who made an impact on Tony's life and whose lives he impacted. As I think about our guys, I ask myself: Who is on their dock? If we saw a scene like this for them, whose faces would be shown? My hope is that every guy in our churches would have a dock full of people. They would have adults parenting them well at home. They would have a church family that cares for them and calls them to a life of worship and discipleship. They would have Christlike parents, grandparents, small group leaders, disciplers, coaches, teachers, youth ministers, friends, and neighbors on their docks. The dock would also be filled with those people that our guys are discipling.

I don't just want every guy to have a dock full of people. I want the dock to be full of the right people. As I am writing this paragraph, I am also mourning another report about abuse that has gone on within a church. The report details the ways a denomination neglected to protect and support abuse victims, including many minors. In our desire to fill the dock, we also must be wise about whom we give leadership positions. Every youth ministry must have child protection policies to protect all of our students, including our guys. We have to be diligent in this area. Every guy also needs multiple adults on their dock who are listening to them and watching for their safety. Every guy needs to know that they have a dock full of adults who will care for them as they go through life. This is especially true if a guy ever experiences any form of abuse. May we be a generation of youth workers and parents who help our guys fill the dock with godly, wise, safe, and caring adults.

5

Rites of Passage

It is powerful when a student graduates high school. Families and friends often celebrate this momentous occasion with balloons, air horns, and signs. Graduation is both a time of celebration and a time of commissioning for the next stage of life. The student's life is categorically transforming. Students have put in a lot of preparation for graduation, going to class, studying, taking tests, and doing homework for years and years. The life of a parent is forever changed as well. Parents have been praying for their children, helping with homework, giving practice tests, and getting them to school every single morning (and as a parent I know this is a grind!). At graduation, this huge accomplishment is celebrated, and graduates are challenged as they head into their next season.

In a teen's spiritual journey, there are various moments youth workers can utilize to prepare and challenge teenagers for the next stage, milestones that we can commemorate. This chapter will look at the purpose of rites of passages and their importance in youth ministry, including specific examples of some of the rites of passages we provided for our guys. As you read, think about your context and specific moments where you might be able to equip parents and challenge teenage guys to live for God in their next season of life.

Purpose of Rites of Passage

Our guys today are at a major disadvantage when it comes to rites of passage because they are not a common part of many people's lives. Rites of passage, though, are so important. They give those who participate a marker of where they are in life. The rite of passage helps him to understand the responsibilities and freedoms that come as he progresses to a new stage, and they help him move on from the previous stage of life. Rites of passage can be formal times like the first day of kindergarten, a thirteenth birthday, or graduation. They may also include things like a child's or teen's baptism, first date, or first varsity game.

Rites of passage help the adolescent male in his movement toward manhood. Developmental researcher David Elkind studied teenagers and wrote about the need for age-appropriate markers. His concern was that teenagers no longer have a clearly defined time to move from childhood to adulthood. Instead, they are forced into adult decisions and issues without a period of preparation. One of the reasons for this is the loss of clearly defined markers along the way to adulthood. Elkind makes the case that these clearly defined markers help to reduce teen stress and angst by helping teen guys understand the season they are in while also not adding stress of having to make decisions that are beyond their years or abilities.[45]

As I talk to youth workers, it's clear that anxiety in teens continues to be a dominant issue. The CDC claims that anxiety is second only to ADHD as the most diagnosed mental health disorder in today's children. Depression is fourth on the list. From 2016–2019, the CDC estimates that approximately 5.8 million children were diagnosed with anxiety and 2.7 million with depression.[46] Farrell and Gray, authors of the book *The Boy Crisis*, write,

> When a boy drives down the serpentine road of mental health, feeling depressed and isolated because he feels no one who knows the real him loves him, no one needs him, and there's no hope of that changing, he may one day find a cliff and drive off. That choice may be direct, as with suicide, or it may be indirect, as in a school shooting.[47]

In 2019, the suicide rate per 100,000 for males aged 15–24 was 22.0 (compared to 5.5 for females in the same range). The rate for males was also a great increase from 3.1 for males aged 10–14.[48] If Elkind is correct that "markers protect teenagers against stress," then creating rites of passage in our ministries may to combat the rise of anxiety in students.

My wife currently ministers to students at a church in an affluent area. These teenagers drive up to church in incredible cars. They have beautiful homes. They have the resources to pursue their desires and dreams. Yet, anxiety is a common feeling among them. A couple of years ago (pre-pandemic), I went as a volunteer leader on their fall high school retreat. On Saturday night, we had the classic retreat share time around a bonfire. Out of almost one hundred high school students, around forty shared. Every single student who shared stated that they had been in or currently were in a time of anxiety, stress, and/or depression. Post-pandemic, anxiety continues to be a dominant part of teens' testimonies.

One of the benefits of a rite of passage is that it clearly defines the stage a student is in and the expectations of that student for that age. A rite of passage also helps adults define how they can be involved at a particular stage in a teen's life.

The rite of passage to manhood is an important part of raising an adolescent guy. In *A Fine Young Man: What Parents, Mentors and Educators Can Do to Shape Adolescent Boys into Exceptional Men*, Gurian makes the case that all males have the need for rites of passage because those celebrations help young men to develop in appropriate ways. If boys do not have these moments, then they tend to create their own rites of passage that tend to be in ways that the community does not approve.[49] While the need for rites of passage is needed in society, it is especially needed in faith communities so that our guys develop according to God's design.

The rite of passage may be a formal ceremony or a gradual transition but must be performed. The church is a unique place for this to happen in our society. So much of our society today isolates generations. We have in our churches one of the last remaining opportunities in western society to celebrate our guys and challenge them for the next stage of life. If we are not careful, we too run the risk of isolating our students from adults in the church. But if we are wise, we will find ways to connect adults to students and celebrate their rites of passage.

Rites of Passage in Student Ministry

In ministry, we have a unique opportunity to connect generations and to equip parents for rites of passage. The first opportunity we have is at the birth of a child. Just this week, our middle school minister and his wife celebrated the birth of their first child. My wife set up a Meal Train for them, and our middle school volunteers have been delivering meals and encouraging them as new parents. The birth of a child is a wonderful thing to celebrate! And the church is not only celebrating with them, but also encouraging/mentoring them in this new role. In our denomination, we do an annual church event called Baby Dedication. We use this time to equip and call parents into their role as primary disciplemakers of their new child, as well as to celebrate the birth of the child.

The church could equip parents for a new rite of passage at the beginning of a child's elementary school years. The start of kindergarten/first grade marks a major change in the daily schedule of a student as well as the beginning of a new developmental phase. At my church, we decided to use this rite of passage as an opportunity to train parents on how to have gospel conversations with their children. We used this time to involve children in our corporate worship services. At the beginning of August, we brought the new kindergarten class into the sanctuary with their small groups. We helped these kids get more familiar with the space and walked them through the order of worship. These incoming kindergartners also got to meet our pastor and other ministers who led from the stage.

In the early elementary stage, many parents struggle with how to lead and parent their children, especially boys, during corporate worship services. When my family was at this point, we were in a unique situation in that my wife and I sat near the front during services with many of our students. When our own four-year-old was about to start attending worship with us, it was daunting to know that we were about to have our new, not fully developed, parenting skills displayed in front of the whole church! Wisely, my wife had a plan. I came home from the office one day to find our living room laid out like a worship service with chairs lined up to emulate a pew facing a TV screen. She had a recorded worship service cued up on the TV. Together, we went through the whole service with our child, pausing the TV before each new worship portion. We explained to our oldest what was about to happen and what he was to do during that section of the service. Practically, this helped him to know when he was supposed to stand up, when he could get his coloring sheets out, when he could leave, etc. Theologically, the exercise gave us a great opportunity to teach him why we worship in the way that we do.

As children approach their teenage years, the church has unique opportunities to celebrate other rites of passage. The start of junior high provides an opportunity to celebrate and commission guys. I always enjoyed making an event of bringing our new junior high students into the youth room for the first time. They would be so excited to get to go to the place where they heard there were pizza, donuts, and ping-pong tables, but when they got there, they would often cower in fear behind me when they saw how big the older students were. Our ministry offered two events to help with this transition. First, we began offering a crossover weekend retreat at the end of summer for our sixth graders before they started their first year in our youth ministry. Our children's pastor would be the primary leader of the event, but he would also invite me to come to portions of it to share about our student ministry and invite them to it. It also gave me an opportunity to get to know the guys before they became immersed in a sea of teenagers in our programs.

One of the things we want to watch for is bullying behavior from older guys toward younger ones. The earlier our adults can get connected to the incoming class or junior high or high school students, the more we are able to watch out for this kind of behavior. Forming relationships early also gives teenagers a connection to an adult they can go to and share if they do experience bullying.

Another event we put together was a back-to-school luncheon for teens and their families. We invited the whole student ministry, taking care to specifically reach out to our incoming families who didn't yet know us well. This event had high parent attendance. Parents tend to have a high interest in this new stage of life when their children are entering the middle school years. Our ministry primarily used this luncheon as an opportunity for parents to network with other parents and to cast the mission and vision for the youth ministry. We cooked a great BBQ lunch meal and gave families time to sit and eat with one another. I then gave an overview of our youth ministry that included the mission of our ministry, the weekly programming that accomplishes the mission, the policies/procedures for teens, and the dates for all the events for the upcoming year. At this event, we welcomed and celebrated the incoming students, inviting and challenging them to spend their teenage years as part of our youth ministry.

My wife does an event just for sixth graders and their parents at our current church where she serves as one of the two middle school ministers. They host a sixth-grade orientation night before they begin any fall programming. At this event, they decorate the tables and hang student ministry banners around the room. They make the place feel like a welcome party. They also give every sixth-grade student a youth ministry T-shirt. They have pizza and eat a cake with the student ministry logo on it. All of the small group leaders are there at the door to welcome the students and their parents. The staff puts out games like gaga ball and nine square in the air for the sixth graders to play. There is also a table laid with all the student ministry information for parents with great handouts and QR codes linking to small group and event signups. After the parents and students hang out and eat, they do a short program that covers introductions, some fun crowd games, and an overview of the upcoming weekly and special events. I love that they also bring a few students who just moved on to high school to talk about what they enjoyed about the middle school ministry, what God did in their lives through middle school, and offer a challenge for the new sixth graders. This event grows every year; in this past year there were almost sixty new sixth graders in attendance! If you choose to do an event like this, my suggestion is to make it fun and high energy, give lots of information to parents (new parents want information!), and challenge them with student ministry testimonies.

For individual families, the thirteenth birthday provides a unique opportunity to challenge our sons as they move toward manhood. I got to be part of a thirteenth birthday for one of our church members. When this kid turned thirteen, his dad rented a cabin and invited his son's grandfathers, children's pastor, and me (youth pastor) to one of the meals. We had a great BBQ meal (can you tell I'm from the South?). After we ate, the dad gave us the chance to go around the table and describe manhood. Even as a thirty-year-old, it was great to hear these older men's stories of manhood and learn from their wisdom. The dad later said that weekend was impactful for his son and himself not just in the moment but also throughout the teenage years. During times of crisis or a major life decision, he and his son would go back to those conversations at his thirteenth birthday.

Graduation is another rite of passage. Navigating this marker well involves more than just attending many long graduations and grad parties (tell me you are a youth worker without telling me you are a youth worker!). Many churches, ours included, also offer events to celebrate graduates. At our graduation event, we tried to accomplish two goals: celebrate our seniors' time in our student ministry and commission them for the next stage of their walks with God. We asked adult men who had a significant spiritual relationship with our senior guys to write letters celebrating and commissioning our senior guys. In the letters, we asked the adults to state qualities and gifts they saw in the student's life and to challenge them to serve God in the future. We asked for letters so that the students could physically take them as they headed into their next phase, whether it was college, work, travel, or something else. Our senior guys especially responded well to this, especially if they had not had men in their lives who encouraged them verbally.

Another thing that we did for our graduating seniors, both guys and girls, was offer a small group series on the transition to college and/or adulthood. Usually around the beginning of March, I would take six to eight weeks and cover topics that would help them finish high school well and prepare them for the next stage. After a few years of doing this, I discovered a general flow that worked well. Seniors are wrestling with identity. A great beginning point for a series like this is to cover our identity is in Christ. The last thing we want is for our students to graduate high school and leave their faith behind. Second, seniors have a need to finish well. Offering a series like this gives us a great opportunity to help them spend their final days in high school with the people who mean the most to them, like parents, siblings, and close friends. Through the series I challenged them to build on those connections, encouraging our students to go out to eat with their parents with the stipulation that there would be no talk about college decisions, scholarship applications, etc. The goal was quality time for parents and graduating seniors without stressors. I also challenged our students to take their siblings out to Sonic or for ice cream. Younger siblings of seniors are also about to go through a major life change and often get overlooked. Third, I used the series as a way to help students build practical skills that would help them in their next phase of life, covering help for the next stage through topics like time management, budgeting, how to succeed in the classroom, managing college relationships, handling roommate conflict, and navigating the weekend. We also invited an accountant to speak to our graduating seniors and their parents about budgeting in college. A great resource for a series like this is the book *Sticky Faith* by Powell and Clark.

When rites of passage are commemorated in our ministries and our homes, they can help our students move confidently toward the next stage of life while knowing that the strong relationships that have seen them through to this point will still be there to lean on as they move toward adulthood.

6

Disciplemaking Around the Work of God

I recently heard a collegiate coach on a talk radio show in Charleston, South Carolina, discussing how little collegiate players today know about baseball players from the past. The coach said that during his childhood, he and his peers collected baseball cards. Dads and sons would look at the statistics on the back of the cards together, trading stories about players they watched games. Today's generation of collegiate players, however, did not grow up with baseball cards. Instead, they're more familiar with social media posts from their favorite current players that occur in real time. This is not necessarily a bad thing, but in this transition the important conversations where one generation shares the stories of the past with a younger generation are lost.

The world is changing at a rapid pace, and it can be an overwhelming task to define and speak about all of the many contemporary problems and issues that male students face. In the frenzy to create relevant curriculum for our youth, we sometimes skip out on teaching about the historical work of the Lord. Over fifteen years ago, Christian Smith described students in his research as following a theology termed "Moralistic Therapeutic Deism." In this theology, youth believe that God wants them to be moral people who are nice to others, God wants them to be happy and feel good, God takes a hands-off approach unless he is needed, and God will send them to heaven if they are good.[50] Students often overlook the work of God in their daily lives, as witnessed throughout human history.

In Psalm 78, Asaph reminds the reader of the importance of one generation sharing the stories of God's work in human history. In doing so Asaph is helping the adolescents of Israel to recognize how God has worked in the past, how to trust Him in the present, and how to become people who will teach the next generation to do likewise.[51]

An Unhealthy Focus on the Future

Today's teenage guys often have an unhealthy obsession with what they will "become" rather than focusing on who they are and the task that they have before them in the present. Veith makes the case that the past has already taken place and the future is directed by God. Thus, the primary importance is what we do in the present, yet our culture is obsessed with things that will happen in the future.[52] Our guys today are constantly pushed toward things in the future such as future championships in their sports while just learning the game, future careers when they barely know how God has gifted them, and future relationships while they are growing in their character and purity.

Although preparing for the future is a worthy goal, today's teenagers need to connect the work of God to their daily lives and their various roles in that day-to-day: as a student, an employee in a drive thru lane, an athlete, a student leader in youth ministry, etc.

Many modern student ministries place a heavy emphasis on the future, which leads to a lost connection with God's work in the past and the wisdom we can gain from it. As youth ministry expert Arzola writes, "radical individualism often leads church movements or fellowships to 'start over again' instead of learning about church history."[53] Instead of learning and building on the past, we in student ministry tend to live only in the present crisis, often adopting the mentality that we always have to create something "new." This has the side effect of isolating teens from the historical work of God both in individual lives and in the church. Remembering and learning from the stories of the past helps us to ground our ministries in the historical work of God and apply it to our present, while modeling to our teens that they can see the God of the past, present, and future at work in their lives today.

An Unhealthy Focus on Spiritual Experience

In youth ministry today we also often see an unhealthy portion of teaching focused on an individual's spiritual connection to God and on their moral behavior, without teaching God's providential work. Focusing primarily on the present can lead us to overemphasize spiritual experiences with God and sometimes results in youth workers spending most of their time on creating large group worship or programs. I love that we've done so much in the past couple of decades to create quality, dynamic worship services for teenagers. I also love our focus on helping teens connect with God in these moments, and I have seen so many students who have experienced incredible life change during times like these. However, I also have seen how our guys have passionately worshipped God in these services and then completely lived outside of God's will during the week.

When I was working full time in youth ministry, I had our students lead worship each week for our midweek service. At the start of each year, I would gather the team together and talk about the importance of how they live offstage. I found this to be one of the hardest struggles in leading a student band. It was easy for them to focus on the performance but neglect the importance of obeying God throughout the week. One of the guardrails that can help students to live a holistic faith is to teach a God who is providential. He is not only present in our worship services, but also providentially working in their life every day of the week. This is something we can continually teach them about and share stories about in our ministries and in our small groups.

On August 27, 2005, my wife and I were newlyweds three weeks into our marriage when we took a quick trip from our new apartment in New Orleans to my in-laws' house in South Carolina. We decided to take a long weekend to go pick up our wedding pictures. (This was back when you had to physically pick up your wedding pictures rather than just get a link.) When we arrived at their house, we found out a storm was heading toward our home in New Orleans: Hurricane Katrina. For the next two weeks, I watched every news station, read every New Orleans newspaper online, and scanned social media posts trying to find out the status of our apartment, my Jeep (which we'd left at home), and our seminary where we were both students. When we were eventually able to return, we found that our ceilings had been so damaged that we could no longer live in our new home. The apartment we had just finished unpacking was lost.

Some lost less than we did, while many others suffered even greater loss in Hurricane Katrina, including loss of life. No matter the size, every loss leads to grief. Our students also suffer losses in their life. Many of them suffered loss during the pandemic, like a senior year of sports or prom. Some students in our ministries will lose friends who move away or lose a pet. Some students will lose a parent to divorce or death. My church ministered to one high school student whose parents both died from cancer. In the midst of these losses, we long for God to write His beautiful story of redemption. This redemption can become more evident to us when we share with others what has happened in each of our lives. In a college class I teach on children's ministry, we spent the whole lesson yesterday talking about the losses in our lives and how God has worked in our lives during and after them. We then discussed how we can minister from a place of loss and redemption, and how we as a team can reach so many more students in their loss because of our collective stories.

In moments of loss and grief, we want to know that God is real, that He is good, and that He is able to meet us where we are. This is the beauty of the providential work of God. The same God who is at work all through the Bible is the God who is with us in our toughest times. During the aftermath of Katrina, we saw God do some of His best work. My wife and I were able to get out of our lease because the apartment was deemed unlivable. My dad purchased us renters' insurance while we were on our honeymoon, and that insurance ended up covering all our losses. God provided places for us to stay while we continued to take classes at, and work for, the seminary we attended. I never would want to live through Katrina again, but I am so thankful for what it taught me about the work of God. I had a front row seat to see God do some of His best work both in my life, in my new marriage, and in the city of New Orleans.

Our guys will face tough experiences throughout their lives. As they move through their teenage years and then into adulthood they may experience difficulty in a marriage, in a job, in parenting, in taking care of parents, in finances, in ministry, or through sickness, injury, or death. Our guys often face difficulties in their teen years, like loss of a friend, family crisis, an injury, school problems, and difficulty in relationships. In these moments, they need to know that they have a God who is able to sustain them. When they have a sense of who God has been throughout history, they can feel the confidence and faith that come with knowing He has done it before and will do it again.

Teaching the Lord of History From Psalm 78

Psalm 78 is identified as a "Maskil of Asaph." A *maskil* is translated in the CSB as a "song of instruction" because of its instructive value or musical difficulty.[54] The psalm is designed to instruct the people and to be used in the liturgy of Israel and is written by Asaph, one of David's chief musicians. This psalm can help us teach the God of history to our guys.

> My people, hear my instruction;
> listen to the words from my mouth.
> I will declare wise sayings;
> I will speak mysteries from the past—
> things we have heard and known
> and that our ancestors have passed down to us.
> We will not hide them from their children,
> but will tell a future generation
> the praiseworthy acts of the LORD,
> his might, and the wondrous works
> he has performed.
> He established a testimony in Jacob
> and set up a law in Israel,
> which he commanded our ancestors
> to teach to their children
> so that a future generation—
> children yet to be born—might know.
> They were to rise and tell their children
> so that they might put their confidence in God
> and not forget God's works,
> but keep his commands.
> Then they would not be like their ancestors,
> a stubborn and rebellious generation,
> a generation whose heart was not loyal
> and whose spirit was not faithful to God
> (Psalm 78:1–8).

Asaph teaches that wisdom is to be passed from one generation to another. Wisdom literature commonly goes beyond conveying wisdom to also emphasize the importance of passing gained wisdom on to the next generation. The psalmist here understands that wisdom connects the past, the present, and the future, and states in verses 3 and 4 that he will teach "things we have heard and known and that our ancestors have passed down to us. We will not hide them from their children but will tell a future generation." Our guys need this kind of wisdom to live in the present. We can learn from the psalmist that some of the best wisdom comes from listening to previous generations.

The psalmist claims in Psalm 78:2 that he will share "wise sayings" and "mysteries." Historical psalms are designed to not only relay what happened, but to inform and transform the recipients.[55] Just as Jesus used parables to share truth about the kingdom of God, this psalm has the potential to teach us.

While modern men seek "new" information, the psalmist states that he would speak "wisdom from the past" (78:2). As Goldingay writes in his commentary on Psalms, "Israel knew that wisdom more often lies in what has been passed down through the generations than in the latest theory or research finding, which will soon be outdated."[56]

In Psalm 78:5 Asaph says, "He established a testimony in Jacob and set up a law in Israel, which he commanded our ancestors to teach to their children." The goal of disciplemaking is that the disciple will trust and obey God and that the disciple will be able to teach the next generation to do the same. While current education practices tend to focus heavily on individual learners and their future, the psalmist understands the importance of teaching wisdom over multiple generations.

Asaph writes that wisdom is passed from one generation to the next through generational discipleship and states in that these are "things we have heard and know, and that our ancestors have passed down to us" (Psalm 78:3) and "they were to rise and tell their children" (Psalm 78:6). In Deuteronomy 6:6–9, parents are instructed to share the story of the work of God in their lives and to teach the *Shema* (Deuteronomy 6:4–5) through the rhythm and ritual of their daily lives. In this passage the psalmist echoes these claims for parents and extended families to pass on the teachings of the work of God. As Mays writes, "the speaker views the people of God as a family whose identity and ethos are maintained across generations because parents tell children the story of how they came to be the people of the Lord."[57] The end goal of telling the story was that the next generation would put their "confidence in God," not forgetting "God's works," and keeping "his commands" (Psalm 78:7).

Even though today's generation of younger guys have incredible access to the Word of God, there is still a great need for one generation to share the works of God to another. As Paul wrote in Romans 10:14–15,

> How, then, can they call on him they have not believed in? And how can they believe without hearing about him? And how can they hear without a preacher? And how can they preach unless they are sent? As it is written: How beautiful are the feet of those who bring good news.

In Psalm 78 Asaph provides a liturgy for the people of Israel to use. He details the Israelites' wilderness journey (78:12–39) and an extended account of the years from Egypt until the choosing of David as king (40–72). This narrative in two parts was not recorded for historical record but to be "recited or chanted as part of the liturgical agenda of religious assembly."[58] This liturgical usage is designed to show the historical work of the Lord and to remind people of the dangers of neglecting God's work and active rebellion.[59] The psalmist acknowledges the importance of parents in the home and the community of faith in worship services sharing the *same* story.

Youth ministries today should pay careful consideration to the teaching elements of our services. We tend to heavily focus on the connections students have individually to God and to each other. But do our teens know the character of God and the work of God through human history? Do they know stories like how God rescued the Israelites from Egypt, how He established a covenant with them, how He gave them food in the wilderness, how He gave redemption to Rahab, how He gave them land, how He sent them into exile, how He protected them while they were in exile, and how He brought them back to rebuild? If they don't know stories like these, God will only be someone they meet with once a week in youth ministry programs. If instead we regularly tell the stories of how God has been at work throughout history, they will see the character and work of God in a grander sense and look for Him to do similar things in their own lives.

There are many ways we can go about sharing the long history of God's work with younger generations. My son's fifth grade teacher spent the first few months in their Bible class having students fill out a short journal that traces God's work from creation to the fall to redemption to the final restoration. This practice has helped my son so much in seeing the big picture. Many of our guys have a similar need to know the stories of God. The students in my college classes continually tell us teachers that they wish they had gotten more theology in their youth ministries. Youth ministries can help teens get a better understanding of theology by periodically teaching through the whole story of the Bible. A few years ago, in the student ministry I led, I took a year of teaching to go through the story of the Old Testament. For each story of the Old Testament, I tied it into a passage of the New Testament. As I taught, I also made a point to give context to the passage so that my middle schoolers and high schoolers would have a better understanding of what was happening. I also tried to share one or two things they may not know about God or themselves that would correspond with each passage.

Another thing I did periodically was read books by great faith thinkers. It can be challenging to find options that will be a good fit for teen readers, but going through a book together can spark great conversations. Memorizing Scripture or basic statements of faith is another way we can help our guys gain a better understanding of the timeless, always-present nature of God.

7

Disciplemaking Through Family Ministry

My mentor, Dr. Allen Jackson, took a trip to Israel about ten years ago. While he was in Israel, he bought me a mezuzah as a gift. The mezuzah was a small wooden case with a small scroll inside the case inscribed with the words of Deuteronomy 6. The mezuzah is intended to be placed over a front door as a reminder to live out the Shema. When my wife and I moved with our kids from Mississippi, the last thing I packed up was the mezuzah. When we moved into our new home in South Carolina, the mezuzah was the first thing that I put in our house. It serves as a reminder every time we leave or return that we are to love God with all our heart, soul, and strength.

The mezuzah represents something I think we should all keep in mind as we minister to teenagers: We need to begin by equipping their families to put God first.

Biblical Foundations of Family Ministry

The practice of ministering to an adolescent's entire family has its roots in the Old Testament Scriptures and New Testament theology. In Deuteronomy, 6:5–7, Moses instructs the people,

> Love the LORD your God with all your heart, with all your soul, and with all your strength. These words that I am giving you today are to be in your heart. Repeat them to your children. Talk about them when you sit in your house and when you walk along the road, when you lie down and when you get up.

God created the family to disciple kids into mature believers. As Paul David Tripp writes, "God intended the family to be his primary learning community, parents to be his primary teachers, and family life to be just the right context for life instruction to take place."[60] We can take lessons from Scripture as we think about how to apply this wisdom to today's families.

In Deuteronomy 6, parents are instructed to "teach" God's commandments to their children and to "talk" of them during teachable moments in the day. For us today, that could be over breakfast, on a walk together, in the car on the way to practice, or before bed. Deuteronomy 6 also instructs parents to state the commandments and teach young people the meaning and application of the commandments through their daily experiences. Parents at that time were equipped and held accountable to teach their children in the daily, weekly, and annual activities of their homelife and their religious community. As Lawson states, "No one has ever devised a more comprehensive education system to empower parents in their responsibility to raise children."[61] The Old Testament concept of family went beyond just the parents to include extended family and the religious community. All three groups were responsible for instructing children.

While the Old Testament explains the specific daily responsibility of the family in teaching children the commandments, the New Testament speaks more in generalizations. The family in the New Testament is a picture of the Father's relationship to the Son and Christ's relationship to the Church. The family is to represent these relationships to a lost world in the way fathers and children interact and in the way husbands and wives interact. In the area of religious education, the New Testament broadens the responsibility of instruction to the church as well as the parents. In passages such as Ephesians 6:1, children and parents are given instruction alongside one another. Paul charges fathers in Ephesians 6:4 to "not provoke your children to anger, but bring them up in the discipline and instruction of the Lord." The New Testament affirms parents as primary disciplers of their children and the church as responsible for providing mature believers as teachers and pastors to family members.[62]

Role of Youth Ministry and the Family

A youth ministry misses a major opportunity to disciple teens when it focuses only on the church and not the family. "The influence of the student's family on his or her value system will exceed the influence of the youth worker on most occasions,"[63] Senter wrote in the late '80s, words that remain true today. In Deuteronomy 6:5–7, Moses instructs the family to be a community that learns and lives out theology. This community is meant to be a place not just where Scripture is mentioned or God is referenced, but where the Spirit and teachings of God influence everyday actions. As Tripp writes, "To theologize with your teenager does not mean that you are to throw in an occasional Scripture verse that relates to the topic at hand. Rather, it means that every day, in every way possible, to embed the story of your teenager in the larger story of God."[64] My kids go to a Christian school and every week they are assigned memory verses. We practice these verses every morning as they go to school. I do this on the way to school for two reasons. One is to help them memorize the verse for their grade. The bigger reason is that it gives me an opportunity to ask them if they understand what it means. Through their answers, we can then discuss how it applies to them in their school that week. It also gives me something to recall when difficult moments happen throughout the week.

Just like a plane needs two wings to fly, youth need both the church and their family to grow into mature, lasting faith. As Smith concluded from The National Survey of Youth and Religion, adolescents' religious lives most likely will mirror the religious lives of their parents.[65] We must avoid clipping the family wing, and instead look for ways to encourage and support the family's involvement in developing teenagers into mature believers.

Many Christian parents understand this responsibility for the spiritual lives of their children. In a study of 278 parents from thirty-six evangelical congregations, over 90% rejected the statement "Ministers or other church leaders are the people primarily responsible for discipling my children and teaching them to share the gospel with others."[66] However, 20% of parents "never read, studied, or discussed God's Word with their children," and 35% of parents have not "engaged in any family devotional or worship time" in the last two months.[67] The survey concluded not that parents expect the youth minister to be the primary discipler of the children, but that parents were too busy to make spiritual development a priority and that the church was not properly training parents to disciple their children.[68] These studies make it evident that parents often know that they are responsible for discipling their children but many are too busy or simply don't know where to start. Part of our role as youth workers is to continually encourage parents to disciple their own children, equipping them to succeed in this calling.

Even as we call and equip parents to be the primary disciplemakers for teen guys, we want to acknowledge the important role of the church in a guy's life. The Bible speaks to the importance of other adults as essential to the spiritual development of students. Adolescent guys need their immediate family, but they also need the family of God. Our churches and youth ministries should provide places where our guys gather with brothers and sisters in Christ, are loved by the church family, and are discipled by other disciples alongside their parents.

Designing Family Ministry for Disciplemaking With Guys

Some researchers and authors claim that the best way to disciple guys is to get rid of youth ministry. The thinking is that youth ministry drains resources from the church, separates teens from their parents, and is not producing results. A major flaw in this argument is that many youth ministries are trying to partner with parents in ministry, equipping them to disciple their children. At the same time, it's not the case that all parents are well-discipled and prepared to disciple their children, or all have a strong desire to do so. More and more parents are claiming no religious affiliation, and the pool of parents able to disciple their children continues to decrease. (In some cases, the patterns are reversed from what we once expected. I know several teenagers who accepted Christ and then led a parent to Christ. The teenager then discipled the parent for a while, but before long God reversed the relationship back to His design of a parent discipling a child.)

The truth is that teens are less likely to grow into a mature, lasting faith if they are only discipled by a parent or only discipled by the church. Both the church and family are needed in long-term faith development.

As we think about the necessity of reaching the family to minister to guys, we youth workers have to realize that it will take time to get there. Before launching a family ministry, make sure to take a moment and assess your current ministry. I had a desire for our ministry to be a place where parents understood their calling to be the primary disciplemakers of their children and were held accountable to it. Rather than jumping into the deep end, I had to learn to take small steps to get there.

Our current reality was that many parents saw our youth ministry as a drop-off service where ministry specialists would teach their children all they needed to live a moral life. To get to a place where parents were ready and able to be their kids' primary disciplemakers, I began by offering parent training sessions. Sometimes we would cover topics like what the Bible teaches about the role of parents and the task of parenting. Other times, we would discuss specific issues such as technology, bullying, or social media. One training parents especially appreciated was focused on how to listen well and ask good questions of their teens. We tended to see the best turnout for the sessions that focused on specific topics parents were encountering in raising teenagers.

The parents had already bought in to our ministry, but I still spent time discipling and training them in disciplemaking. Then these parents began discipling other parents. Parents spend a lot more time with other parents than I realized before I become one myself. Parents spend hours together at games, school events, performances, and the car line. When we help them with their parenting skills or give them a new vision for parenting, they will tell others about it.

I also began finding ways to connect our youth ministry with other ministries in our church, looking for ways to align our teaching and partner together. Through this, we were able to offer teaching topics for adults that connected to what we were teaching teens. I had the unique opportunity (and time-consuming task) of recruiting not only my student small group leaders but also the leaders for our adult small groups, which proved to be another way to build connections between various ministries and what groups were discussing. Creating a family ministry with this approach was a challenging ten-year process, but over time, it had a positive impact on our families.

Equipping Parents for Disciplemaking Their Sons

I remember my first day in my former role as an Associate Pastor for Students. I walked into my new office with a few boxes of books I'd brought along from seminary. I was excited to put into practice all that I had learned in school and all that I had read in those books. As I sat down in my office chair, the phone rang. It was a mom calling because she had found an illegal substance in her son's car and didn't know what to do. I hadn't even been in my office an hour and here was a parent in distress.

I talk to moms and dads often who are looking for help with their sons. I have found that they are often asking for help in three areas: commandments, conversations, and commissionings.

Commandments

Parents are looking for help in understanding what commandments they're holding their kids to. They are often wondering what expectations are appropriate for their teenage guys and how to hold them accountable to those rules without pushing them away. Youth workers can be a great asset to parents in this area. We want to challenge parents to set appropriate boundaries but to do so in grace and truth, according to the example God provides. Youth workers are connected (or can quickly get connected) to a network of experts in many of the topics parents have questions about, which can help parents in these areas. Parents will show up to trainings if they see the need to learn the information we are giving. This is the main difference between adults and students. Students will often show up for the event for the social opportunity, adults show up for the information. If we can determine a few things that parents are struggling with in parenting their teenage guys—such as social media/ technology usage, bullying, worry/anxiety—and find experts to speak in these areas, we can be a huge resource for parents. As youth workers, we can challenge any speaker we bring in to talk both about teenagers as a whole and about specific issues that they face. We can then wrap up the session by speaking about the issue through the lens of the Bible.

Conversations

Many parents want to know how to have better conversations with their teenage guys. Often we think about girls when we say "conversation," but guys are also in need of continual conversations with their parents, especially conversations where parents say things like "I am proud of you," "I love you," and "I am here for you." Many parents struggle with how to do this.

We've all seen this scenario: *Parent: "How was your day?" Son: "Good."* End of conversation.

We can help parents by teaching them how to ask good questions. Instead of asking "how was your day?" parents can be more specific and ask what was one really great thing that happened and what was one thing that wasn't so great. This forces the guy to reflect on his day and also to give real examples. Another way we can help parents have more conversations with their sons is by encouraging them to do things together. As mentioned in the male learning theory section earlier, guys' brains are engaged during activity. Engaging in conversation while our bodies are active can be hugely beneficial. There are so many things that we can do with our sons that give us opportunities to have conversations together: fishing, painting, sports, workouts, video games, watching movies/tv, traveling, and the list goes on.

Commissioning

Youth workers can also help parents by commissioning those parents to disciple their sons. In turn, parents can commission their sons to the call that God has placed in their life.

I love coaching my youngest in flag football. One thing that I noticed on the field is how many parents show up to watch their sons play. I honestly get a little jealous of how many parents rec leagues can attract. I also love that parents show up for other activities guys are involved in—band, acting, choir, equestrian, etc. One of our challenges is to help parents recognize their call to spiritually lead their teens and be as involved in that aspect of their life as they are in their sports or extracurriculars. I think one of the reasons that we often see parents helping their sons in sports is because they know the sport, and the coach gave them practical ways to practice at home. They know what to do: They have knowledge to give and a plan to follow. We should learn from these lessons from sports and work as a church to disciple parents and give them a plan to disciple their sons. I will give more specifics in later chapters on how we can do this.

A related task of parenting is commissioning sons to follow after God in their adult years. One motto we use at the college where I teach is "Your Purpose. Our Mission." Many guys today are in search of purpose and meaning. Even though God gives all of us the responsibility to help guys discover their purpose, He often first uses the family to reveal it. Parents are in a unique position to first see the way that God has uniquely created each guy. It is powerful when a parent shares with a teen what gifts they see in their son and calls them to use those gifts for God's glory. As a collegiate professor, I have seen firsthand the difference it makes when a guy comes into college confident of who he is and where God is calling him.

Part III

Rallying to Developmental Needs

As the wall was being rebuilt, Nehemiah began to see the needs of the wall and the needs of those who were building. He saw that enemies were plotting to frustrate their work. Nehemiah's response was to bring the people of Israel even closer together to continue the work. Nehemiah stated, "The work is enormous and spread out, and we are separated far from one another along the wall. Whenever you hear the sound of the ram's horn, rally to us there. Our God will fight for us" (Nehemiah 4:19–20).

As guys enter adolescence, they are beginning a journey of unique developmental needs. Nehemiah reminds us as spiritually discipled adults not to abandon our guys during this time but to "rally" to them. Rallying begins by seeking to know our guys and where they are in their development and spiritual maturity. We then surround them with spiritually discipled adults ready to minister well to them. Finally, we call guys to take the next step in their walk with God and prepare them for future steps.

8

Guys in Middle School

Middle school is a unique time. Guys enter middle school looking like kids and leave looking much more like teenagers. I have spent the last four years serving in our church's youth ministry as a small group leader for middle schoolers. When my current group were sixth graders, I felt like a professional cat herder. Through their seventh-grade year, I felt like a drill sergeant. And now that they are in eighth grade, I feel like a coach preparing them for the next stage of life. My experiences with them have reminded me of the importance of adult leaders during this crucial development stage. As middle school guru Mark Oestreicher wisely writes, "These days, we see high school ministry as being 'corrective' in nature, while middle school ministry is now the make-or-break space (or 'preventative' in nature)."[69]

Chap Clark uses the illustration of a tightrope. The poles of childhood and adulthood are relatively stable forces, but in adolescence a student walks out on the tightrope in a journey of independence.[70] As a sixth grader, the adolescent male is taking the first steps of this tightrope walk. This beginning point of adolescence is coming earlier and earlier. Puberty can start as young as ten in boys today, with growth spurts for boys occurring as early as ten as well. While the starting point of adolescence begins with a biological marker: the beginning of puberty, the end of the tightrope concludes with a social marker: the full acceptance of adult responsibility.

Because today's boys are stepping onto the tightrope of adolescence earlier and earlier, they now exit middle school near the tightrope's center. And the longer the tightrope becomes, the more it bounces in the middle like a swinging bridge. Clark writes,

> An increasingly lengthy adolescent process makes the concept of familial separation for the postmodern early adolescent a far different, and more difficult, experience than it was for his counterpart a century or even a generation ago. Postmodern youth workers need to be aware that in a culture where few systems and relationships are trustworthy or stable, adolescents need to know that a Christian ministry designed to serve them will do all it can to ensure an experience of stability and health.[71]

This does not imply that we as youth workers usurp the role of the parent. We are called to serve our students as they walk this tightrope by being stable forces in their life. As Paul mandates, we are to be "self-controlled, worthy of respect, sensible, and sound in faith, love, and endurance" (Titus 2:2).

We can minister well to middle school guys as we rally them. As we do so, we need to be watchful of early and late maturers. We also need to think about how we teach middle school guys. We need to think about leading a middle school guy small group well. And finally, we need to aim at shaping well the heart of a middle school guy.

Time of Rapid Change

Physical development is one of the most noticeable and impactful changes that takes place during a guy's middle school years. The first eighteen months of a child's life are marked by rapid physical change (hence the month-by-month photos many parents take). After those eighteen months, the rate of change decreases. That rate of physical changes ramps back up in early adolescence. For guys, the growth spurt during this period can add twelve to thirteen inches to their height. Around the same time as the growth spurt is occurring, adolescent guys also experience the development of secondary sex characteristics including change in voice, broadening of shoulders, facial and underarm hair, and sweat-producing glands and acne. For parents, the emergence of stinky sweat in their child can be a traumatic experience! I remember going to a seventh grader's house for a weekend retreat. The smell, comprised of seventh grade boys, Axe body spray, and Cheetos, was overwhelming. The host home parents just quarantined the guys upstairs and deep cleaned after they left!

Boys notice these physical changes in themselves and others in their middle school years and may have a wide range of reactions to these changes. One of the struggles for ministry to guys is the wide range of when physical development begins and ends for individual students. On average, boys may start or end physical changes up to two years later than girls. And the range of first appearance for body growth can start anywhere from ten and a half to sixteen years of age. Early- and late-maturing have benefits and difficulties for guys. The benefits of being an early-maturing guy are usually related to more opportunities for sports and leadership. The early-maturing guy is usually significantly bigger than his peers and gets an increase in playing time. The early-maturing guy also often gets leadership opportunities in class and in social situations because he looks older and more mature than his peers. A difficulty for the early maturing guy is often that though he is seen as older than he is, his emotional and mental development are not there yet. He may be given lots of opportunities due to his appearance but may not have had the life experience or age to prepare him for them. Because he may seem older in certain aspects, the early maturing boy may also be exposed to older students and risky behavior at a younger age.

The late maturing guy often faces difficulties that have lasting effects on his well-being, like struggling with self-confidence. He might be at a higher risk for bullying behavior.[72] And even though a late-maturing guy may end up being taller than his peers by late adolescence, he may still be bullied for being short during this season. Regardless of how he compares to his peers by the end of adolescence, the fact that he was shorter and smaller than his peers at one time can be hard to shake.

The late-maturing guy may also miss out on opportunities for leadership or skill development because he does not get as many practice hours as early-maturing boys. Malcolm Gladwell highlighted in his book *Outliers* that the overwhelming majority of professional hockey players were born in January, February, and March because in Canada, eligibility for child hockey leagues begins in the month of January. A close birthdate to January gives a significant size advantage to a child and results in more playing and practice time. Gladwell states that while an athletic boy might start out a little better than his peers, this divide grows when he is given multiple practice and playing opportunities while his younger peers are not. Over time, this divide grows exponentially.[73] While we see this happening in sports, this can also happen in our student ministries, especially in leadership and discipleship opportunities. We want to be aware of this temptation so we do not overlook what God wants to do in certain guys—like David being overlooked at first by Samuel while David's older brothers were presented as candidates to be king.

Late-maturing guys may have as much talent as early-maturing guys but might be outpaced simply because of the opportunities given to the early-maturing guys. I have had several conversations with dads my age who said they and their wives decided to hold their sons with summer birthdays back a year after reading Gladwell's book!

Late maturity may also come with some benefits. A late-maturing guy may get more information about their developing bodies and be given more time to slowly grow into their teenage years. A guy who is late maturing may also be shielded from risky behavior until the decision-making part of his brain has had more time to develop.

Ministry Implications

One of the hardest things about skiing is learning how to walk to the slopes in those uncomfortable boots. As a teenage guy begins to go through rapid growth, there are going to be some awkward moments. It may be his voice changing or his body changing from short and stocky to long and muscular. And all these changes can occur at varying rates. The task of the parent and youth worker during this stage is to walk alongside each guy, giving him information and helping him back up when he slips and falls.

First, we want to offer empathy to the student during this time of rapid change. I had a guy once go from not getting a lot of notice in sixth grade to being the tallest and strongest in his class in seventh grade. He then became a major distractor in small group. I quickly grew frustrated with his behavior. But after learning his story, I found out that he had rapidly grown in the past year and didn't know what to do with all the new attention that he was getting because of it. I still had to help him manage his behavior in small group, but I approached him with a lot more empathy than I had before finding out about what he was experiencing and where his behavior was coming from.

Second, student ministries should surround middle school students with adults who will offer them accurate information and support. As Walt Mueller writes, "Most of these changes occur during the middle school years, when group acceptance is of the utmost importance and when peers—because of their own impulsivity and insecurities—tend to be the most cruel and insensitive."[74] As adults, we tend to have more information and can deliver the information and support to a middle school student in more helpful ways than his peers can. We can come alongside them and help them know that they're not alone in what they're experiencing. As Oestreicher and Rubin write, "We're convinced that one of the most important ministries you can have with young teens is to normalize their experience."[75]

Third, we should repeatedly teach and model to our guys that their worth comes from who God says they are. Guys today struggle more with body image than they have in previous generations. We want to make sure our view of the guys in our group does not start with their maturity, personality, physical presence, or skill, but with the fact that they are created "in the image of God." Because they are created in the "image of God" (Genesis 1:27) and have been "remarkably and wondrously made" (Psalm 139:14), we should show honor and value to each guy in our ministry according to their inherent worth as God's creation.

Finally, we must continue to be mindful of early and late maturity. Just like in sports, it can be easy to give leadership opportunities to early-maturing guys. We must seek to disciple each teenager specifically where they are in their journey with God and not just focus on the early-maturing guys. We desire for each student to find his place in the body of Christ and develop his gifts and ability. As Paul wrote, "Instead, God has put the body together, giving greater honor to the less honorable, so that there would be no division in the body, but that the members would have the same concern for each other" (1 Corinthians 12:24–25).

Youth ministries should also be watchful for bullying behavior and to create safe spaces. At my previous church, we instituted a no bullying and no pranks policy. We saw that most pranks were aimed at late-maturing guys, and many "pranks" began to rise to the level of bullying. It can be especially hurtful to a child when he is bullied as much (or more!) at church as he is in school, athletics, etc. The atmosphere of a welcoming, familial, safe space must be established and reinforced by the adults in the room.

Teaching Middle School Guys

In addition to physical changes, intellectual changes that have a big impact on kids during their middle school years. I love the mental descriptions that Reggie Joiner and Kristen Ivy give for a kid's different life stages in their book, *It's Just a Phase So Don't Miss It.* As an elementary-age student, children think like a scientist. Scientists love to make observations with their senses and test out all possibilities of the observed world. In middle school, students begin to think like engineers. Joiner and Ivy describe middle school students as engineers because they take their learning from childhood and begin to create, connect, and build into new ideas and subjects, like algebra, robotics, and theater.[76] Adolescent guys are beginning the process of developing abstract thinking. They are not there yet—as we will see in the chapter on disciplemaking with high school guys—but they are starting to develop this skill. In middle school teens begin to have abstract thoughts, but they quickly ground these thoughts to concrete reality.

In the elementary years, guys tend to be later in developing their reading ability than girls. In addition to girls hitting puberty a year or two earlier than guys, we also see evidence of this intellectual delay in our ministries. Many of our middle school guys are still thinking in literal, concrete ways. Many are also still catching up in their reading ability. In teaching middle school guys, I have had to learn some teaching techniques that allow them to think literally about the text while also stretching them to begin thinking abstractly.

When we teach the Bible to a group of middle school guys, we are teaching an ancient text with an unchanging message. However, we are teaching this ancient text to a student who's in the early stages of a period of hyper-change. For the unique stage of middle school, we want to teach the message of Scripture to someone who thinks like an engineer and who is gaining the ability to think abstractly. I have found that asking questions, playing a game, using an illustration, and telling a story works especially well for teaching Scripture to a middle school guy. This approach also works for a middle school girl—but I have found that I usually need more ideas planned for our guys' groups than our girls' groups. I've also learned through teaching middle school guys who think like engineers that it's important to be very clear in connecting the opening activity to the text we are studying. I always write out my transition from the opening hook moment so that I am very clear about that connection because I know it will impact my guys' overall engagement.

To reach guys best, we as youth workers should ask a mix of questions both about the text we are studying and about their daily lives. This combination allows teens and pre-teens to think abstractly through the application questions while being grounded by the questions about the text that are more concrete. In my middle school guy groups, I start by asking plenty of questions about the text, often in the form of who, what, when, and where questions. For example, tonight I taught 1 Thessalonians 2 to my group of eighth grade guys. For verses 3 and 4, the questions I asked about the text were: "Who is Paul aiming to please?" (God) and "Who is Paul NOT trying to please?" (man). These are two great questions for middle schoolers because they helped guys get to the heart of what the text was saying. Observation questions are good because they are questions that a concrete learner can find and answer in the text. These kinds of questions also allow me to inspect their understanding of the text. Sometimes middle school guys are accurate with their reading of the text … and sometimes they are way off.

After making sure guys understand the text, we want to help them apply the text to their lives, still primarily through concrete questions like who, what, and how. For the lesson in 1 Thessalonians 2:3–4, the three application questions I asked were: "What are some examples of how people seek approval from others?" and "Have you ever backed down from something you believed in or taken a different stance in order to gain popularity with a particular group of people? Explain," and "How would your words and actions be different if you lived to please God and not man?" Application questions like these allow guys to think hypothetically and connect the text to their real-life situations.

In response to these questions related to 1 Thessalonians, we had a great discussion in our group on ways that middle school guys wrongly seek approval from their peers, like fighting not out of anger but to impress their peers.

Finally, we always want to end a lesson with transformative questions that ground abstract thoughts to actionable steps in thc coming week. Sometimes I will call this section "So what?" especially if the lesson has been heavy on abstract concepts. When I am teaching a mixed group of middle schoolers and high schoolers, I am always thinking of the transformative section with my middle schoolers in mind. I do not worry about going too far with abstract concepts for high schoolers with middle school students present because I know I will ground the middle school guys back to reality at the end of the lesson.

Managing a Small Group of Middle School Guys

With developmental changes in overdrive, middle school guys tend to have the most behavior problems in small groups around seventh grade. In talking to many small group leaders and youth ministers, and learning from my own experience, the middle school years are when behavioral issues tend to be at the highest, but they also set the framework for future behavior in small groups. My current group of guys had a rough seventh grade year with lots of behavioral problems. It was a long year teaching, but then they made a turn as eighth graders and we had an incredible year. Almost all of the guys shared at the end of the year that small group was their favorite part of middle school ministry. They liked that time each week to gather together with Christian friends, share with one another, and learn from God's Word.

Managing a small group with middle school guys begins with honoring and valuing them as created in the image of God. I once had a middle school guy in my Bible study who had a lot of behavior problems. It was easy for me to label him as a "bad kid" and seek ways to get him out of my group. When I began to ask questions about his home life, though, I found out that his dad was in the process of leaving the family and moving out of the house. I thought about this guy's identity from God's eyes. I remembered that he was created in the image of God. This teenager was living in a fallen world, a world in which his father was abandoning the family. He was also a child going through the roller coaster of emotional development. And he was also someone who needed to know and experience the gospel for himself.

With all of this in mind I began approaching him in a different way. I decided to value and honor this young man. I offered empathy to him by asking him questions about his life and listening to his answers. I wouldn't just label him as a "bad" kid, then ignore him and invest my time in the "good" kids. When my co-teacher taught, I would go sit by him not only to monitor his behavior but also to encourage him when he answered a question correctly or participated in a way that was good for the group. I held him up to the same standard as everyone else, but I also sought to not abandon him by warmly greeting him each new week regardless of his behavior the previous week. I made it a point to talk with him any time I saw him outside of our group setting. And I prayed for him, lots.

Managing a small group of middle school guys is only successful when youth workers and volunteers have the right motivation. It can be a tough balancing act to set a safe and respectful tone in the room and continually monitor for appropriate behavior while not losing the mission of the ministry. Sometimes, leaders prioritize group management above all else. When this happens, the group may run smoothly but students stop showing up. Although the group is managed well, the disciplemaking mission is lost. Another pitfall is focusing only on the lesson and not on classroom management. For myself, I've noticed that I tend to ignore behavioral issues and just keep teaching. But though when I do this, I think I'm focusing on the gospel, the unintended consequence is that the gospel is not reaching every student. The students who are being disruptive are not hearing the message, and the students who are more mature are not hearing the message because they are being distracted or frustrated with the others. Learning group management is worthwhile because it helps every student to be able to be reached with the gospel.

Group management is not something that comes naturally to all of us but is a skill anyone can get better at. This is very true for male small group leaders who have never had experience leading a group, especially a group of teen guys. Small group leaders often tend to be either too lax or too harsh in group management. These tips can help: 1) make it a point to greet each student at the door, which establishes a relationship from the beginning of the lesson. 2) small group leaders should also find ways to talk to every guy and not just their favorite students. Students pick up things like this and may act out either out of hurt or for attention. Students are also more likely to participate throughout the discussion when they know that their small group leader notices them and cares about them.

Small group leaders are responsible for the pace and tone of the group. Before I walk into a group, I check my attitude. Am I ready to lead with a welcoming and encouraging tone? When I have had a rough day, I have learned not to try to hide it (which is never successful anyway—teenagers always know). Instead, I have grown to realize that I need to be honest and tell them that I have had a rough day. Interestingly, I've found that when I am honest and forthright in this way, guys often start sharing about their own tough days, or sometimes they stop and pray for me.

Small group leaders should also have a few clear group rules and enforce them well. I sum up my rules with one statement: "Have fun when we are having fun. Be serious when we are serious." Teenagers often will get these backward. Our guys will disengage when we are doing an activity and then be disruptive when we study the Bible. I challenge them to reverse this. I ask them to go all in with fun when we do an activity and be serious when we engage with the creator of the universe and the savior of our souls during worship and the reading of His Word.

There are times when a small group leader will need to enforce rules with a disruptive middle school guy (that is also true for girl groups, but

I have found that our guy group leaders need to be especially trained in this area because they have to use these skills more than our girl small group leaders). I like to think of dealing with behavior issues as green light, yellow light, red light. Sometimes, I have even put the lights on screen in order to show the group where things are. When a student is disruptive, student ministry leaders should first ask him to stop the behavior. This is a green light moment because he can continue in the group but just needs to be aware of his behavior. If the behavior continues, then we move into yellow light. Often, simply moving a guy to a new seat away from his friends will stop the behavior. I will often move him right beside me, especially if my co-leader is teaching. If the behavior does not stop, then we may move to red light. At this moment, the student may need to be removed from the group for the night or for a couple of weeks. For this to work, youth workers need to be available during small group time so that he or she can talk to the student away from the group and call parents if need be. I was always hesitant about this step, fearing that I would drive the disruptive guy away. Over time, I have found that the overwhelming majority of disruptive guys will come back and often this was the step that they needed. Also, if I didn't remove the continually disruptive student then I risked my core students becoming frustrated and finding other groups or ministries. It's important to note that the youth worker needs to welcome the student back when they return after being removed. The student may be hesitant to return but the leader taking the initiative to invite him back is worthwhile. And then if the leader greets him at the door, this will often do even more in the guy's maturity than even the act of removing him from the group (which probably happens often in other areas of his life). Even better is if you as the leader can call the student the week that they can return and tell him that you are excited about him coming back. This often will minimize the hesitancy to return.

Finally, I have also found that a guy's behavior usually improves when leaders spend time with him outside of the group. When we put time into the relationship with guys, they tend to want to be more participatory in small group. Spending time with your small group does not have to be a huge ordeal. It can involve playing ultimate frisbee, frisbee golf, or backyard sports. It can also be just meeting at a fast-food restaurant before or after small group. Just like when you invest money into a bank, we want to invest time into these relationships. We then stand a better chance of the student participating during our small group time, and we let the student know that we are someone it's safe to turn to as they continue to grow and learn in faith and in life.

Shaping the Heart of a Middle School Guy

One way we make disciples of middle school guys through making sure that that they clearly understand the gospel. (A quick aside: much of this chapter and the next chapter applies equally to disciplemaking with girls; but I've chosen to include it for two reasons: 1) It's critical understanding for effective discipleship, and 2) Since this is a book about guys, that continues to be my focus here.) As we teach the gospel, it is not uncommon for middle school guys to wrestle with their walk with God. Often, this inner conflict stems from their growing skill of abstract thought. They are able to think about God in new and unique ways. This is where youth workers and other adult mentors can come alongside them in their doubts, listen to them, and share the truths of the gospel with them. One skill we have to learn as disciplers of middle school guys is to listen and ask questions well. Often, middle school guys struggle with putting into words what God is stirring in their hearts. Be patient. Listen well. Ask questions to help them learn to put their own thoughts, doubts, and curiosity into words. This helps to create a pathway from our heart to their heart.

We also need to help middle school guys connect to the larger family of God. We want them to build relationships with faithful adults and people of multiple generations in the church. We also want to connect them with a friend group that is seeking God. Although parents are still the primary influencers in faith and values through the teenage years, teenagers spend significant time with their friend groups, and these friend groups have a high impact on their decision making. We want to create places where groups of friends who seek after God are formed. Small groups are a great place for this to happen. We'll look at this in more detail in the last few chapters.

9

Guys in High School

One summer at a camp for high schoolers, I was leading a group during devotions. The guys in my group began to share that they wanted to stop letting their phones take up so much of their time. I offered to help in any way, even by keeping their phone for a bit. I offered this more of a gesture, not really expecting anyone to take me up on it. About two weeks later, though, I was sitting in my church office when one of my senior guys came in and asked me to hold onto his smartphone. My first thought was, *what did I just do?!?*

I called his mom to come get his phone. To my relief, she was happy with his decision and said that they were on the way to get him a temporary flip phone so that he could still get and make calls. A few weeks later, the senior guy asked me, "Have you ever heard of Matt Chandler and Francis Chan? I have all this time without my phone, and I have been listening to their sermons on my computer." His discipleship took off. Our conversations about spiritual things went much deeper. He also used his afternoons to help at the church and gather donated soccer supplies (jerseys, cleats, etc.) for an international mission trip to Africa.

Guys in high school can go much deeper in their walks with God than we often give them credit. In school, some are studying calculus, reading early British literature, performing chemistry experiments, memorizing lines for theater, and practicing for hours to perfect their athletic or musical skills. They get frustrated when they go to church and it's a few songs, a shallow message, and one adult doing all the work. They may not use the word "frustrated," but they do vote with their feet. They enjoy our ministry, but they are being asked to do much more in school and other places where they are given opportunities to lead and perform, and those are usually the places they are drawn to.

At the same time, we have to remember that high school guys are still developing teenagers. In 2018, Red Gerard won an Olympic Gold medal in snowboarding slopestyle. On the biggest stage of his life, he became the youngest snowboarder to win gold. Yet, he had almost missed the event because he stayed up late watching *Brooklyn Nine-Nine* on Netflix the night before. He overslept and then couldn't find his jacket. His roommate had to loan Red his own jacket so that he could compete.[77] Is that not the most teenage thing ever? High school guys can accomplish incredible things, like winning an Olympic gold medal … if they can wake up on time and find their clothes.

Teaching to an Abstract Thinker

Whereas middle school guys think like an "engineer," a high schooler thinks like a "philosopher," according to Joiner and Ivy. Philosophers love to ask why something is the way it is and to think deeply about concepts they have previously learned. Philosophers also like to create meaning out of their thinking.[78] High schoolers are known for asking why and searching for meaning and purpose. This move is driven by the transition from concrete thinking to abstract thinking. In abstract thinking, the adolescent begins asking "what if?" This shift changes the way high school guys see themselves, others, the world, and God.

What does this look like in practical terms? Teenage guys become idealists. They are able to think about a hypothetical, ideal world. And when an adolescent compares the world where he lives to the ideal world, they often find a big gap between the two. Thus, adolescents become champions of the ideal and the underdog. Teenagers also become critical of current systems, often focusing on how they are parented. As developmental psychologist Elkind writes, "Now that adolescents have developed formal operations, they can construct ideal parents and compare them with their own, whom they usually find sadly wanting."[79] Not only do guys compare their parents to the ideal parent, but they also compare each other to the ideal guy. The ideal guy can look very different to different people. When they compare, they may begin to ridicule or bully each other. As youth workers and small group leaders, we want to make sure we are teaching that each one of us is wonderfully made by God, and each of us has honor and value. We also want to be proactive in shutting down jokes and words that ridicule others, as well as setting the example of honoring and valuing one another.

Though adolescents become critical of the current world and champion the ideal, oftentimes they struggle in living out the ideal that they claim. They long to see the ideal in their life and world but can sometimes struggle in putting a plan in action in their life to achieve their dreams.[80] One of the tasks of a youth worker is to help our guys not only vocalize their beliefs, but also understand and appreciate the hard work that is involved in fulfilling these beliefs.

Abstract thought allows teens to perceive the world idealistically, and also leads to ideal perspectives on how they can live in an ideal world. With help to pair practical actions with their ideals, teenage guys are able to see their ideal self in the future and determine steps in order to attain this idealized self. This new skill of formal thought helps them to envision what they might want to do with their life and then to begin taking steps to achieve that future.[81] In other words, teens can perceive an idealized world where they can be the ideal parent, worker, athlete, missionary, etc. Sometimes, however, this idealized person leads to a messianic complex. The adolescent sees the need for change to happen and believes they are the only ones to recognize this. And they believe they are the only ones who can accomplish this heroic change.[82] Teens sometimes view themselves as the only one capable of bringing forth the ideal world. As youth workers and small group leaders, we can play a crucial role in affirming and encouraging high school guys in the unique way that God has gifted them. We will often see it before he sees it in himself. We also can play a crucial role in helping him learn to serve God and others with the gifts he has, rather than move forward in thinking he is the one to save the world.

In middle school ministry, youth workers help students to focus on concrete questions like what, when, where, and how. In high school, we should introduce the questions of "why" and "what if?" "Why" questions are important because they allow teens to think introspectively about their own life and beliefs, and also allow them to think abstractly about God. If you are teaching a guys' high school small group, I would challenge you to look back over your lesson and see how many times you asked "why" and "what if" questions. Try adding a "why" question periodically in your lesson and see how your guys engage with it.

In high school ministry, we can invite teens to begin asking questions, leaving space for God to show up in the answers. When leading a group of guys in this stage, it can be daunting to ask these kinds of open-ended questions. We are not always sure that we know the answer. Oftentimes, there is no concrete answer. It helps to go into lessons with a good understanding of the material. Take time before teaching a lesson to read and study the text so that we can help guys find the answers to questions we ask or that they may ask, or simply to sit with them in the unknowns. I love teaching at a Christian university because whenever I have questions, I can walk across the hallway and ask the experts. I also did this on church staff. If I was teaching on a subject that I did not know well, I would go ask our senior pastor or other staff members their thoughts on the subject. I challenge you to do the same. Find people you can ask questions, people who are constantly challenging you to grow. Guys, both teachers and students, can sometimes think that we have to figure out everything on our own. We have a great opportunity as youth workers and small group leaders to model to teenagers the importance of learning from one another. Remember that it is also appropriate to say to a high school guy, "That is a really great question. I would love to think about it and research it. Why don't you do the same and let's get back together and talk about it next week."

We also want to invite teenagers to study Scripture alongside us. In ministry, I have seen far more girl groups read together than guy groups. I challenge you to find periodic times to read a great book together with your high school guys. I always loved the discussions I had with senior guys when we engaged in this practice. Many had never read a religious book before, so it became exciting for them and me. I started doing this later in my time as a youth worker in the local church and wish I had started earlier.

Another thing that we can do with high school guys more easily than with middle school guys is to hang out outside of our formal times together. At the church where I now serve as a middle school small group leader, our high schoolers all go to Chick-fil-A after our midweek small groups. This gives leaders an opportunity to hang out and to continue conversations in smaller groups or individually with students. It's not uncommon to see an adult volunteer and a high school guy talking across the table about the lesson or just life in general. Guys especially need these opportunities because of how few times they have deeper conversations in other areas of their life. They also may not feel comfortable asking some of the questions they have to the large group. You may not have time to meet right after small group, but it's worth it to get together outside of small group, maybe getting breakfast on a weekend or before school, playing a sport with guys from your group, meeting after school at a fast-food place, or doing a mission project together in your community. Of course, make sure to think through safety and security for these meetings outside of regular programming (meet in a public place, never be alone with a teen, etc.). When done well, these times can be great moments for guys to ask questions, encourage one another, think deeper, and build stronger connections with each other and their leaders.

Teaching Individual Grades in High School

Our ministry focus can shift as kids age through high school. For the freshman year, disciplemakers should focus on building the community of the group. The friend group that a freshman chooses is crucial for the future years. As people commonly say, "Show me your five friends and I will show you where you will be in five years." Small group leaders should focus on helping freshmen guys learn about one another, hang out together, and pray for one another, building those important friendships along the way. Freshmen guys are also beginning to think abstractly. This is a great time to start introducing the "why" questions in small groups.

For the sophomore year, disciplemakers should focus on character and godliness in decision making. Sophomore year is when many guys get their driver's licenses. With their license, they now have more control over where they go and what they do. This can create a crisis of belief as they often must choose whether to follow the crowd or pursue godliness. The sophomore small group leader can build off the community established during the freshman year and continue encouraging guys to follow God throughout their high school years.

Sophomore year is also a great time to share case studies with your guys. For example, you might be teaching students on how Jesus models how to serve others, going so far as to wash the disciples' feet. Then, you could give your guys an example of a real-life leader humbly serving others, maybe sharing an example from college sports or the news, a story of a current high schooler, or an example from pop culture. Help guys to draw parallels between the real-life story and the biblical text and example of Jesus. Ask them how they thought most people would react in those real-world situations and how they'd feel going through if they were actively involved, and how their perspective might change if they remembered Jesus' example of humbly serving one another.

After the sophomore year, most guys still in discipleship are committed and have a desire to serve, making junior year an opportunity for disciplemakers to develop leaders. The disciplemaker's task is to first help junior guys discover how God has uniquely created them. Many small group leaders have spent several years with their guys by this time. Over those years, leaders tend to see gifts and abilities God has given each student, often before the guys have themselves. Disciplemakers should help junior guys find opportunities to use their gifts both in the church and in their community. Remember that even if guys do know their gifts and abilities, they often don't know what to do with them. Disciplemakers can open the doors to opportunities, doors that often won't open without an adult volunteer's or youth worker's help.

During this season of high school, guys are looking for purpose, meaning, and identity. These searches are inherently spiritual in nature. They also can lead guys toward idols. What does that look like? Tim Keller asks and answers, "What is an idol? It is anything more important to you than God, anything that absorbs your heart and imagination more than God, anything you seek to give you what only God can give."[83] High school guys struggle with many idols: sports, relationships, possessions, looks, grades, skills, jobs, leadership opportunities, etc. Even though all these things can be good, they can become idols when a guy finds his purpose and meaning from them rather than God. Sports injuries can be devastating because they represent the loss of an idol. Disciplemakers should challenge junior guys to use their gifts while also helping them to not make an idol out of their abilities.

For the senior year, disciplemakers should encourage guys to make a lasting impact on their last year in high school ministry while also thinking about how to serve God in the future. I have found that the current senior class sets the tone for the rest of the youth ministry. If the senior class is engaged, then the rest of the student ministry feeds off of them and follows them. If the senior class disengages, so it goes with the younger high schoolers. The senior guys will often set the example for all the younger guys. I have noticed that senior guys who disciple younger guys leave a lasting legacy. Disciplemakers of seniors should consistently challenge them to lead well.

This week I received a wedding invitation for a guy I had in a small discipleship group during his high school years. It brought back a lot of memories. I remembered him being a part of a large group of energetic freshmen. I remembered how during his sophomore year they began making the decision to follow God rather than the crowd. I remembered his junior year when he and his friends began leading backyard Bible clubs for children on mission trips, leading student worship in our student band, serving in our corporate worship services, and leading their campus ministry groups at school. I especially remember his senior year when he and his friends began reading the Bible with some seventh-grade guys. The legacy that group left lasted for many years, and future groups imitated them. This is the kind of thing that can happen when we disciple guys well through their high school years.

One Final Note: Reach Every Guy

Although there is a general developmental plan that God has designed for guys, there is also quite a bit of variety. Some guys start a stage earlier than others and some go through the stages more quickly or slowly. As we lead small groups of guys, it's helpful to know the typical developmental stages but also crucial that we remain flexible. When guys are slower to progress through the stages, we should be patient with them and find ways to help them grow in their next steps. We also want to be proactive in making sure that others do not ridicule them. One area to watch is when we ask our guys to read the Bible out loud. I usually ask for volunteers to read first. If someone may be slower in his reading, I make sure to shut down any ridicule quickly. There will often be at least one person in a given group with a learning disability, so it's important to make sure that our group is a place that shows support and love for one another.

One of the best ways to set a good tone for a group is to establish a group covenant at the beginning of the year, with teens and leaders agreeing that we will listen when someone is talking, we will encourage others, and we won't tease or make fun of one another.

Some guys have disabilities. We want to make sure that our room and our lessons are accessible to all. One of the things I wish I had learned earlier on is to be proactive in making our rooms accessible. We should make sure that our facility is handicap accessible from the parking lot to the small group rooms. When our facilities work for people with different capabilities, we often will start reaching students we don't even know we are missing. It's also important to reach out to parents of students with disabilities. I too many times waited for them to reach out to me. I found that when I reached out to them first, it showed love for them and their kid and a willingness to learn specifics about their child and how best to minister to them. We should make the changes that will enable us to minister more effectively. Sometimes, this may be changing the layout of our facility, changing rooms, or modifying parking places. Sometimes this may mean creating a space or group just for special needs students. And sometimes this may mean bringing in a special helper for the student so that they can participate well with the group.

Finding ways to reach every student in our group brings so many benefits not only for the individual student but for the group as a whole and even for us as leaders. I had one guy with special needs who couldn't wait to come to our student ministry because we offered pizza and had a student worship band. He tolerated my teaching—but only so that he could worship. He was such a great example to all our students of what passion for worship looks like. Although we might tend to think we are ministering to a student with special needs, often that student is the one who ministers to us.

Within our groups we'll also likely see a variety of learning styles. Some guys learn well through activities and games. Some learn through reading. Some learn through a logical flow in our teaching. Some learn through introspective activities, and some learn through group activities. Some learn through creative expression like music and art. I have found that many small groups cater to one specific type of guy, with many of them being geared toward the outgoing, athletic kid. Our questions are often aimed at those who will speak up quickly. And our activities are designed for those who are most athletic. I've learned that I am much more effective at reaching every kid in my group when I vary my teaching methods. Sometimes I will play a worship song and let teens reflect on the lyrics. Sometimes I will start our time together with a competitive game. Sometimes I will bring in a visual aid. I may also have them journal or discuss a text as a small group. Sometimes I have my guys draw or create a cartoon. When we vary our teaching methods, we may discover a gift a guy's gifts. This provides a new way to help teens become encouraged, get connected, and grow in their leadership ability.

Part IV

Disciplemaking Through Ministry Programming

After the walls were rebuilt, Nehemiah gathered the people of Israel together. When the people had gathered, "They asked the scribe Ezra to bring the book of the law of Moses that the Lord had given Israel" (Nehemiah 8:1). The people gathered together, Ezra read from the sacred text, the people worshiped, and they confessed their national sins.

We are made to gather together in the church, study God's Word, grow in our faith, confess our sins, and worship God. The final section of the book will highlight how to apply adolescent male learning theory to the typical programming of a youth ministry in order to disciple guys. We'll look at disciplemaking in the home, small groups, closed discipleship groups, and missional/vocational leadership training.

One of my favorite teaching books is *Small Teaching* by James Lang. I love the way he organizes his individual chapters. For each chapter, he presents an introduction, a section on learning theory, four or five models of small teaching approaches, principles for creating small teaching strategies, quick tips, and a conclusion.[84] I used a similar organizational approach for the following chapters. Youth ministries already have programs to reach guys. I don't believe youth workers have to tear everything down and start over to disciple guys. What I want to provide in this last section are some small research-based practices that youth ministries can implement in their existing programs that create big results. I conclude each chapter with one big idea that would take a semester or more of work to implement.

As you read through this section, you may see some things that would apply equally to girls as well as to guys. I hope this will be a resource that student ministers can give to both seasoned veterans in student ministry and to new leaders of guys small groups/discipleship groups. Thus, I will include some basics of discipleship for the new leaders that would apply both to females and males. At other places, I will highlight methods/practices that I have found work exceptionally well with groups of guys.

There are many aspects of discipleship, for both females and males, that are not included in this book. What I have included are aspects of discipleship that I have found through my research and observed in my own discipleship of guys that tends to correlate with healthy discipleship of guys. These tools will help us to have more meaningful interactions with guys and encourage them as they grow as disciples.

10

Disciplemaking in the Home

Through my college and seminary years up until we had kids, I worked for a youth summer camp as a Bible study leader and camp pastor for almost ten years. Those years were formational for me as a minister and gave me the opportunity to preach to upwards of 7,000 campers in the years that I worked a full summer. This summer, I got a brand-new camp experience: attending camp as a chaperone with my son as a camper.

The camp we attended was a missions camp where students went to a mission site every day. We were assigned to help organize a thrift store. At the end of each day, the students had a few moments to shop at the thrift store. Some boys found baseball cards. Some found games they bought. My son found the coolest set of penguin salt shakers. Side note: letting guys visit a thrift shop can give you great insights into their unique personalities!

Later that day, my son came up to me devastated that he had dropped his ceramic penguin salt shakers and they had broken. The theme for the camp was "In His Image." That day, we had talked about "Image: distorted." In that moment, I was able to connect the theme of Scripture that we are created in God's image, yet are also sinners in need of restoration. The next day, the theme was "Image: restored" and we talked about how we were going to reglue the penguins back together. Once we got home, we glued them together and they sit on our display case as a reminder of the restoration God does in our lives. Although I have loved preaching to thousands of teenagers at camp, this moment of connecting God's story to my son's life will always be special. And this is the opportunity every parent has with their sons: connecting God's story to everyday moments.

When I began leading a youth ministry in Mississippi, one of my core goals was to find ways to equip parents to disciple their teens. I had been reading family ministry books and taking family ministry classes in seminary. I was eager to find ways to equip parents as primary disciplemakers in their homes. One semester I decided to do a study with dads and their sons. I was really excited about the study and sent out several rounds of invitations. I also invited some solid men in our church to sit at tables with students whose dads might not be able to come. I bet you know how this turned out. I had around twenty teens show up … and two dads. Luckily, the additional men I had invited came and we had some good discussions in small groups for the rest of the semester. Still, I struggled to figure out why there was such a low turnout. I knew we had many dads who were leading their families well, so why did they not come?

Fast forward ten years from the small group study where guys did not show up to the point when I started coaching my son's flag football team. And guess what I found there in plenty: dads! They were watching practices, cheering at games, and helping in lots of different ways. I have nothing against dads cheering on their sons in athletics, but my desire was to see dads and moms be even more effective in the discipleship of their child at home. This chapter seeks to understand how we can equip parents, especially dads, in the spiritual journey of their children. We will look at research findings in family ministry and then look at small changes that can result in big results.

At the same time that I was associate pastor to students/discipleship at this church, I was in the middle of my Ph.D. studies in youth ministry. I saw a need for research on how guys learn and on the impact of youth and family ministry models and practices on the spiritual development of guys. I developed a study on the relationship of family ministry models and practices and faith maturity in teenage guys. I then sent surveys to collegiate freshmen at three different Christian universities in the states of Mississippi, Alabama, and South Carolina. The surveys included a test I developed where these collegiate freshmen guys would choose a descriptive statement that best matched the church they attended during their high school years and then they would answer a series of questions on specific ministry practices of that same church. The descriptive statements described four different family ministry models: family-free youth ministry, family-based youth ministry, family-equipping youth ministry, and family-integrated youth ministry.

The collegiate freshmen also completed the questions that correspond with The Faith Maturity Scale developed by Eklin and Benson[85] From interviews and surveys with theological scholars, denominational executives, and several hundred adults Belkin and Eklin determined that mature faith includes eight core dimensions. From these eight core dimensions of faith, Benson and Eklin produced the thirty-eight questions that measures faith maturity.[86] A person's place on the faith maturity scale is determined based on the responses to those questions.

I chose the Faith Maturity Scale as a baseline for analysis because it tested for the priorities and practices of a vibrant and life-transforming faith. I also liked it because it focuses on two themes and eight core dimensions of faith. The first theme, the vertical theme, is a "life-transforming relationship to a loving God." The second theme, the horizontal theme, is a "consistent devotion to serving others."

The eight core dimensions of faith includes components that seeks to model a student's relationship with God, such as trusting God for salvation, integrating faith into daily life, and growing in relationship with God through spiritual practices. The eight core dimensions also include components of faith that seek to model their practice of faith in the world, such as being part of a caring church community, seeking change in the world, modeling faith values, and serving others.[87]

A person exhibits a mature faith when both themes and all eight areas are present in their life.

Research Findings

In my study of family ministry and male faith maturity, I looked for ministry practices that correlated with faith maturity in teenage guys. For those who are interested in the specifics of the study and the findings, I have included some of the pertinent results in the appendix. One great finding was that all of the family ministry models I looked at correlated with a moderate faith maturity score according to the Faith Maturity Scale.[88] Timothy Paul Jones proposed that the three dominant models of family ministry are family-integrated, family-based, and family-equipping ministry.[89] I studied these as well as a fourth family ministry model: the family-free. I highly recommend reading Jones's book to learn more about these models.

Even though I was glad to see that all the models correlated with a moderate faith maturity score, I was also interested to learn whether any specific ministry practices correlated with a higher faith maturity score in teenage guys. One practice that I studied was the impact of significant spiritual talks at special moments (thirteenth birthday, entering the youth group, driver's license, first date, graduation, etc.).

I was encouraged by the number of spiritual conversations parents had with their sons during significant moments (82% responded that these conversations happened "at least sometimes"). When parents regularly have significant spiritual talks at special moments, their teenage guys tend to have a higher faith maturity score. Parents should be proactive in having these kinds of talks at key moments—the more conversations the better. As Paul David Tripp wisely states, parenting is not one big conversation but many small conversations.[90] We as youth workers can continue to encourage and equip parents to have these conversations at big moments and follow them up with many conversations in day-to-day life.

Another question I asked in my study was, did your parents lead family worship times or family Bible study at your house? Over 75% of participants responded that their families never or just sometimes had family worship times or Bible study at their homes. The high percentage is not surprising. Jones stated that the second factor in the infrequent practice of parents discipling their children was that parents were too busy to make spiritual development of their children a priority. Jones also found that 35% of parents have not offered family devotional or worship time in their homes in the last two months.[91] Almost half of the participants (45.9%) in my study responded that their families never had family worship times or Bible study at their homes. This is another area where youth ministries can equip parents.

This led to my asking another question: To the best of your knowledge, did your parents attend parent training events offered by the church you attended during your teenage years? Eighty-eight percent of guys responded that their parents only sometimes or never attended parent training events. This number is extremely high. One possible explanation could be that teenagers are not aware of the training opportunities that are offered to parents by the church they attend. A more likely explanation is that churches may be family-based in some ways but are doing a poor job of equipping parents. Jones found that one of the two main factors in the low practice of parents discipling their children was that the church was not properly training parents to disciple their children.[92]

I was also interested in fathers' involvement in teenage guys' spiritual lives. I asked: Did your father take an active role in your spiritual growth during your teenage years? Only 43.6% of participants had fathers who always or often took an active role in the adolescent male's spiritual growth during his teenage years. It is encouraging that over 40% of fathers were actively involved in this way, still, there are still many fathers who were not. Those fathers who are active in discipleship need to be involved in coaching other fathers.

Small Changes ... Big Results

Every church reaches multiple generations. Paul makes it clear in 1 Corinthians 12 that every generation is valuable, and every generation is needed to complete the body of Christ. Many churches already have ministries aimed at reaching parents, like adult small groups, adult discipleship groups, and corporate worship designed for adults. From my research into guys and family ministry, I found a few small changes that we should make in order to see big results in our guys.

Every parent disciples their children. I had a sixth grader come one Sunday morning to small group wearing a polo shirt, shorts, and high "Trump" socks. I immediately knew that his parents were big Trump supporters. Every parent disciples. The question is, in what ways are parents going to disciple their kids? Are they going to disciple their sons in sports, performance, academic achievement, politics, relationships, or in Christ? We can help equip parents to make some small but significant changes in their parenting so that they disciple their children wisely.

Commission and Equip Parents for Significant Talks During Special Moments

One small change that we can make is commissioning and equipping parents for significant talks during special moments in a guy's life. Out of all the practices that I studied, significant talks led to one of the biggest differences in faith maturity between guys who had parents who always had these conversations and parents who never had these conversations.

A little prep work in this area can yield big results. First, youth ministries can take some time to plot out typical rites of passages in the lives of guys. Then we can think through ways that we can equip parents for each of those rites of passages. For some significant moments, this could look like us developing a simple resource for parents. For instance, I created a driving contract parents could use with their teens when they started driving. For other moments, it could be an event that parents are encouraged to have with their children, like a thirteenth birthday party. For other moments, it can be impactful to host an event for families at church. In my years as a professional youth worker, I hosted an annual back-to-school luncheon for the parents of our new seventh graders. I also hosted several events for our graduating seniors to help prepare them to live out their faith in college. The goal is to help parents celebrate moments with their sons, have conversations, and allow the Holy Spirit to use those times to challenge their sons to live well and flourish in these new stages of life. Every parent disciples—so let's point them in the right direction.

Utilize Deuteronomy 6

We can also challenge parents to utilize the four opportunities listed in Deuteronomy 6:7: "Repeat them to your children. Talk about them when you sit in your house and when you walk along the road, when you lie down and when you get up." For parents who struggle to have conversations with their sons, this chapter suggests regular moments through the day that we can naturally use to start conversations.

Many parents think that family Bible study must look like a Sunday School lesson or seminary class. I used to think that way myself. But as I read Deuteronomy 6, I noticed that the call was to teach who God is and what He has done in the regular rhythms of life. We've tried to incorporate this in my family. In the morning, my boys and I review and discuss their weekly Bible verses for school. While we are in the car, I have learned to turn the radio off and have conversations with them about their day. These are moments that I was missing because I didn't think of them as opportunities for conversations.

At night, my wife and I have begun a simple process with our kids. Every night we write our prayer requests in a notebook. Everyone has a chance to state his or her prayer request for the night and then we pray over the requests together. This simple practice has already yielded big rewards. One of the first nights, my oldest son stated that he wanted us to pray that his school would not be so stressful. We didn't even know that he was stressed out at school. He broke down in tears when we asked what was going on. My oldest had been stressed throughout the day but we had not given him the opportunity to share his feelings with us. Writing down prayer requests presented a new chance to connect and share. Many nights we pray for simple things that are taking place the next day. All types of prayer requests are okay. The practice creates a pipeline so that when there are big things happening in our kids' lives, they have a safe place to share.

One of our highest goals should be to help parents see the necessity for continual conversations. Paul David Tripp reminds us that parenting is less about big, mountain-moving conversations and more about life-long discipleship.[93] He challenges us to think in terms of "one unending conversation."[94] We as parents can often worry about getting everything right in one big conversation with our kids and forget the power of continual, consistent conversations every day. Utilizing the four moments of conversations in Deuteronomy 6 helps us to live out that one unending conversation with our sons.

Offer Small Groups for Parents of Students

One final small change is to offer small groups for parents of students. Again, all parents disciple. If parents are mature disciples, then they tend to spiritually disciple their children. As Smith and Denton concluded in their national study of teenagers and religion, "We'll get what we are.'"[95]

I have found offering small groups for parents is one of the best ways to train parents. Whenever I offered a parent training event, the only parents who would attend were the ones who were already discipling their children. I still offered specific parent training events one to three times per year because the parents who came had networks of friends who were also parents of teens. Parents love to talk with other parents, and I knew if the training we offered was worthwhile, the parents who attended would share what they learned with other parents. I also knew that many parents were struggling with parenting their teenage sons. If I could help my core parents by offering counseling and training events that offered valuable information and resources, then they would share this information with their network of friends.

In small groups, we can reach many more parents over a longer period. Some of our parents are already in small groups. Some of our parents are looking for small groups. And some parents we may reach with a parent-training event that leads them to want more connection with other parents and training in parenting. I led a parents of students small group the last two years of my ministry before leaving to work as a professor. I absolutely loved teaching this group of parents. It gave me the opportunity to interact with parents who were not volunteers in our ministry and to learn about the struggles and wins parents had with their teenagers. I taught with a man who was retired and had grandkids in our ministry. He brought lots of wisdom and perspective to the group because he had already gone through the season of parenting teens.

The groups we offer for parents of students can be taught in a variety of ways. One idea is to study the same Scripture with parents that their teens are studying. We can then challenge parents to have conversations with their kids about what they were learning throughout the week. Another approach is to study a topic that relates to parenting. I recently led a group on parenting using Paul David Tripp's book *Parenting*. We had great discussions on the role of parents from a biblical perspective. Many of those who were involved in that small group still talk about how it transformed their parenting vision and practice.

One of the greatest gifts we give parents when we read the Bible together is we allow them to see the metanarrative of God's Word and how that relates to their opportunity to disciple as parents. God is the One who is writing the story of not only the world, but your boy as well. He has graciously invited us into the role of parent. Shaping the heart of a boy would be impossible on our own. God, however, invites us into this role with the promise that He will work through us.[96]

This passage emphasizes to parents that they are not "owners" of their kids but are an important "tool" to be used by God. I have sat with many parents who are at a loss with what to do with their teenage sons and the choices that they are making. The conversation always shifts once they realize they are going to have to trust God with the results, that He is the Father watching for the prodigal son.

Spending time understanding and discussing the metanarrative of God's Word also helps parents to see their sons accurately. As they study the Bible, parents are reminded from the beginning of Genesis that their sons are created in the image of God. Whereas today's culture encourages parents to judge their sons in comparison to other guys, God's Word reminds them that every son is born with honor and dignity, created in the image of God, given a purpose to live a life that flourishes. God's Word also reveals that each of us is born with a sin problem. One of the realities parents must understand is the underlying sinful nature that is driving bad behavior.[97] Then the metanarrative in God's story points to the need for redemption. Our sons don't need us as parents to save them or mow down all the obstacles in their life, as many parents today tend to do. Our sons need to know that their only hope for restoration is through the salvation God offers. God's Word also teaches that sanctification is the work that God does in His children. Thus, parents are called to parent with grace and truth to help their children grow more and more like Christ. Finally, God's Word teaches that ultimately Christ will return. While today's culture often teaches that the goal is to have a son who excels in a sport or in the classroom, a parent's goal is not to get them in the right college but to prepare their sons for this ultimate moment.

One Big Idea

One big idea to take away from all of this is to develop a three- to five-year action plan to take your family ministry model from where you are to where you would like to be. I teach a change and conflict management class, and one of the key things we talk about is to be honest about where we are and where God is calling us to be. The tension between these two points creates urgency. We must help our churches see a true reality of how we are ministering to families and a vision of how God wants us to reach families.[98] Often, we try too quickly to look like another church we admire or switch to the latest model we learned at a conference without thinking through the reality of who we are and how to get there. The quickest way to kill the design of a family ministry is to push people into it too fast. I took a five-year approach of beginning first to offer a few parent-training events each year and then slowly building to a model of family ministry where our staff team and key leaders were working together to empower parents to lead their families spiritually from birth to graduation.

We must begin with being brutally honest about where we are as a ministry and its effects on our guys. Then, we should study the Bible, read books, and pray about where God wants us to be in reaching families and sons. The tension between these two realities creates urgency among our leaders to create a plan to get us from where we are to where God wants us to be.

With fellow staff members and volunteer leaders, we can then begin by taking an honest look at how families and our ministries are reaching and discipling guys. Then, discuss with fellow staff members and key leaders where you would like to be in three to five years. Finally, map out a plan to get from the current reality to God's vision.

11

Disciplemaking in Small Groups

As I mentioned at the beginning of the book, I was struggling with leading my small group for guys on Sunday nights. My wife and our female leaders were having great discussions and lessons in their groups, but our small group for guys was struggling. As I researched more into male learning theory, I began to rethink how I was teaching my core guys. We had a fun activity at the beginning and application time at the end, but the majority of the lesson was heavy on lecture and small group discussion. My guys were struggling to pay attention, especially on a Sunday night.

Male learning theory tells us that boys do well with experiential learning. Their brains have been wired to learn through doing; historically, they have been trained in apprenticeships and not in all day classroom lectures. With this in mind, one spring when I had planned to teach the story of Joseph, I got a crazy idea and went to our children's pastor. I asked if he would be okay with my guys writing the curriculum for kids' camp from the story of Joseph and coming up with the daily themes. Amazingly, he said yes (though who wouldn't want to have someone else come up with all the curriculum?)! He allowed my guys to host the morning onstage time and to lead the small group discussions.

The next Sunday, I went to my guys and told them that we had the opportunity to develop the theme, small group lessons, and on-stage activities for kids' camp. The stipulation was that they needed to be present every week for small group. They would need to focus during our study of Joseph so that they would be prepared to develop the theme and small group lessons. They were all in! As we studied Joseph, the guys focused so much better on the story because they knew exactly how they were going to use what they learned. It also gave me a chance to teach them about important things like leadership, how to teach a lesson, what it means to teach yourself first, etc. These guys were motivated. They produced a great camp and learned a lot more about Joseph's life than they would have in a typical group.

Research Findings

One of the questions that I sought answers for in my study of collegiate freshmen was the impact of Bible study groups for teenage guys and how it affects faith development. I wanted to know if groups for teenage guys tended to help or hinder faith development. Especially with the push from some sectors for Bible study to only take place in the home, I wanted to see if there is a significant difference for those who attended Bible study groups with teenage guys and those who did not. My study with collegiate freshman guys who had some level of church involvement found a significant difference between those who attended a group with teenage guys and those who did not. The average faith maturity scores increased the more that a student spent in Bible study groups with teenage guys. The lowest average score was those who never attended Bible study groups with other guys their age. All of this indicates that there is some spiritual benefit for teenage guys to be in a Bible study with peers. In healthy Bible study groups with other teenage guys, a guy can build relationships with guys who will encourage him in his walk with God, sit under biblical teaching that helps him live a godly life, and live with some level of accountability.

While I understand the theological reasoning in some models of churches to moving all of Bible study for children to the home rather than in the church, I am concerned about the loss of specific teaching to this season of life for a guy and the loss of community with his peers.

Paul took a group of guys with him when he traveled. He poured into these guys and eventually sent Timothy and Titus out to pastor churches. We can see in the Gospels that teenage guys need places where they gather together, build community, and collectively learn from wise adults.

In my study, I tested to see how many students had attended Bible studies with their parents and if these family Bible studies had a significant impact on them. Over half of the participants (57.7%) never attended the same weekly Bible study group with their parents. This was the highest number of "never" answers that I found in all of the questions asked. But those who always had Bible study groups with their parents (10.5%) showed a significant increase in faith maturity score. The mean indicated something similar to what I saw among those who always attended Bible studies with teenage guys. What this tells me is that Bible studies, whether with teenage guys or with their family, make a difference in the life of a teenage guy. My recommendation is to offer Bible studies for both groups! Regardless of our model of family ministry, we should all find times for students to study the Bible with fellow teenagers and find times for students to study the Bible in family groups. While our adult groups and student groups met at the same time, the one place that I did see teenage guys study the Bible with their family was when families would go on mission trips together. These were powerful moments not only because they were doing missions together, but also because they were worshipping and studying God's Word together.

Small Changes ... Big Results

Recruit, Develop, and Release Male Leaders

With the need for small groups with teenage guys, one of our primary tasks will be to recruit, develop, and release male leaders. One of the struggles youth ministries have in reaching teenage guys is a limited supply of spiritually mature men who can invest in the lives of teenage guys. The task for developing male leaders is especially crucial today, and is something we will have to do continually, not just at the start of each school year. Our pastor loves to say, "What gets scheduled gets done." If we want to develop male leaders, it is something student ministers are going to have to schedule into their weekly work.

At my previous church, our entire next gen team came to a point where we simply did not have enough volunteers, especially males, to lead our small groups. We gathered in a staff meeting with our senior pastor and expressed our concern. Our staff team began to pray about what we needed to do to develop and deploy leaders. We came to the honest reality that our main problem was simply we did not have enough men who were spiritually ready to use in our ministries. We then began to create an action plan to develop leaders.

Youth ministries need to have spiritually mature men among their leadership—not just available men. All people are created to disciple, and all disciple for good or ill. Some may disciple about sports, working out, art, superhero movies, alcohol, or music. If we desire for men to be disciplemakers, then they first need to be spiritually mature disciples. My former church began creating discipleship groups for men with the goal of molding spiritually mature disciples. We believed that the byproduct of this would be a host of new leaders, and that is what we saw. It took a couple of years before they were ready to be released into ministry, but once they were, one of the first places where many of these new leaders served was in in our youth ministry. As youth workers, discipleship is worth the time because the payoff later is exponential. Although it's typically expected that youth workers will make quick changes and produce quick results, developing leaders is one area where we want to slow down. Discipleship is much more like a smoker than it is a microwave.

In addition to investing in these men through our church's discipleship groups, I began to block out two to three hours on my weekly calendar to work on leadership development and encouragement. Currently, I am a volunteer middle school small group leader. One of the things I appreciate about our middle school youth workers is that they take time each week to email the adult team about the upcoming week. Our middle school guys minister also makes phone calls to encourage us male leaders and takes us each out to breakfast or lunch once a semester. When I was a youth pastor, I spent two to three hours each week calling prospective leaders, preparing training videos or conferences for our team, and encouraging our current leaders. All of this must be in a youth worker's weekly schedule.

It's important that we also rethink the onramp into leadership positions. Early in my ministry career, I would wait until just before the fall semester to start calling potential leaders. Imagine getting a phone call from a pastor saying, "Hey, we need someone to teach a group of eighth graders an hour Bible study every week for the next year starting ASAP. You interested?" That's a quick no. The better way is to invite leaders to observe a small group and then be mentored by a seasoned leader. Imagine this call: *"Hey, I have noticed some things in your life that make me think you would be a good teacher for our guys. God is doing some amazing things in our groups for guys, and I would love for you to be a part of it. I have a great leader for you to work with. You could sit in his group and observe for a couple of weeks. After that, we can talk about if you would be interested in being mentored by him. What do you think?"* This second phone call has a much greater chance of success.

Implement Experiential Teaching

When we teach the Bible to teenage guys in small groups, we want to avoid two tendencies. The first tendency to avoid is teaching only through lecture. As we've looked at, the male brain is not wired to learn exclusively that way. Lecture involves heavy word usage, and the male brain generally does not respond well to teaching that requires sitting still and listening intently. The other tendency to avoid is active learning that doesn't have a foundation of Scriptural truth. Instead, we want to aim at the middle road of teaching the truth of Scripture through teaching methods that activate the male brain.

Paul stated to Timothy, "All Scripture is inspired by God and is profitable for teaching, for rebuking, for correcting, for training in righteousness, so that the man of God may be complete, equipped for every good work" (2 Timothy 3:16–17). Paul affirms that God's Word is authoritative. It is what our guys ultimately need. Through the teaching of the Word, guys' lives are changed so that they will be "complete, equipped for every good work."

In 2 Timothy 3:16–17, we also see that teaching Scripture involves active work. It's not just giving guys verses to memorize but involves teaching, rebuking, correcting, and training in righteousness. These verses are full of active verbs. Engaging lessons lead to Scripture producing changes in the life of the learner. Our lesson plans should include active teaching methods like games, stories, journaling, drawing, discussions, brainstorming, case studies, demonstrations, polls, group work, and minute papers (where students pause for one minute and write an answer to a question). Youth workers will be better teachers for guys when they start with the main idea of the passage and explore it through an active learning strategy that will best engage students with the concept. A simple online search will give you all kinds of ideas for active learning. What you come up with may not be a neat and tidy process, but it's effective at connecting with students. When I once taught an eleventh and twelfth grade Bible study, the room was an absolute mess by the end of the lesson. After all the students left, another teacher walked into my room and asked, "What happened?" I responded, "Learning."

It's common in youth ministry to use games and group activities in teaching. One of the reasons games and activities are effective is that they are fun for students, but they also provide an opportunity for students to actively engage in the lesson and give us as teachers a variety of options for debriefing what they've experienced. We should be thoughtful in how we use games and activities, though, following a few key guidelines. First, we should be wise with how we use competition. Competition is a great motivator, but we should avoid labeling students winners and losers. We should encourage every student because the goal is not to award a winner but to engage every student in the learning activity. Second, small group teachers should use a variety of games and activities to engage students with a variety of gifts and abilities. There is a tendency in guys small groups to focus on athletic competitions. While we have athletic guys in our groups, we also have guys with creative minds, musical talents, linguistic ability, entrepreneurial spirits, etc. When we offer variety through our activities, we allow every guy an opportunity to be a leader and use their gifts. Third, small groups leaders should only use "challenge by choice" in games and activities. In other words, we should never force a student to do something if they are not choosing to do so. We also want to be careful to prevent any type of embarrassment or bullying to a student during an activity. Embarrassing a student is deeply detrimental to the health of a small group. Finally, small group leaders should always write out a clear debrief guide for any game or activity. It is so easy to miss the point of why the game or activity is being used. I always write out the debrief guide to remind myself why I chose what we're doing, which also helps me clearly state the purpose to my guys.

A few other simple active learning techniques I love to use are large group discussion, small group discussion, pauses for reflection, journaling, and case studies. In teaching a lesson, small group leaders should consistently ask questions of the group. Large group discussion encourages teens to actively listen and gives the teacher an opportunity to diagnose learning in real time. Through student answers in real time, teachers can assess their understanding of God's Word and its application to their lives. I have found times when teens are really tracking with me and other times when they have totally misunderstood a story. I then can pause the teaching and correct their understanding.

The problem with large group discussion is that the teens who think the quickest and like to talk tend to dominate the discussion. That is another example of why it is important to use a variety of simple active learning techniques. In a smaller setting, small group leaders can pause their teaching and ask students to silently reflect on a question. Guys who are deep thinkers love this time to pause and think, especially if they are in a group of talkers. Sometimes, small group leaders may want to break the small group up into smaller groups of two or three guys to discuss a question. I have had some groups that are silent when a question is asked to the large group but love to discuss ideas in these smaller groupings.

I remember leading a group of senior guys at camp during church group devotions. The guys would not talk in our group time. I was so discouraged the first night and ended by asking them to pair up and pray for one another. An hour later they were still talking and praying! I could not believe it. For whatever reason, that group of core guys responded better when they were in pairs. As we lead individual groups, we discover over time how our group learns best. Each group is different. That is why a variety of simple active learning techniques should be utilized.

Integrate Brain-Based Learning Theory at the Beginning or Ending of Lessons

One thing science is teaching us about learning is the importance of the first few minutes and the last few minutes of teaching time. The beginning of the lesson and the last few minutes are some of the most strategic times we should utilize because those minutes can maximize learning.[99] At the beginning and ending of a group meeting, we want to employ strategies that help guys remember what they are learning and have learned. Studies have found that collegiate teachers can raise student grade averages by a full letter grade by simply utilizing multiple-choice quizzes at the beginning and ending of classes and periodic quizzes before exams.[100] We can use a more casual version of similar tactics with our groups of guys.

When I was a full-time youth pastor, my small group leaders and I realized how little we did to help our teens remember what they'd learned. We spent lots of time teaching the lesson, then quickly wrapped up with an application before leaving. The next week, we would launch right into a new lesson. I assume this is the dominant teaching method in small groups for guys. It is no wonder that teenagers (and teachers!) struggle with remembering lessons from one week to the next.

We can help our guys remember what they are learning by holding them accountable to the application we suggest for each week's lesson. As the old saying goes, "You can only expect what you inspect." In our ministry, students were not applying the lesson to their lives, so we created a new rhythm for the week that brought about a huge impact. At the end of the lesson, our small group leaders were clear on the application point for the week. Then, our leaders sent the guys in their group a reminder in the middle of the week of what they'd discussed in small group and encouraged them to put the application point into practice. The application of the lesson might be to share what they learned with a parent or friend, read the passage each morning for the week, pray a certain prayer on their way to school, or to serve their friends at school in a certain way. Finally, each new small group gathering started by reminding students of the application of the previous lesson and giving them the opportunity to share how they applied the lesson or with whom they shared the previous lesson. This simple weekly rhythm greatly increased the number of students who were actively practicing the lesson in their daily lives.

It also helps to discover what previous knowledge a teen has about the lesson. A great way to do this is to utilize the K-W-L method of teaching. In K-W-L, the small group leader seeks to learn what the student already "knows," "what" the student would like to learn, and what the student has already "learned."[101] So often, small group leaders simply launch into the week's lesson without assessing what teenagers already know and what they would like to know. Small group leaders can begin the lesson, especially when they're about a familiar passage, by asking teens what they already know about the biblical text. Then, the leader can ask what they would like to learn. These two questions help the leader to know what they can quickly cover in the lesson and at what points to slow down and focus. The K-W-L method creates internal motivation for teens to learn things that they do not know. At the end of the lesson, the leader asks what they have learned, giving students time to reflect on and remember what they're talked about.

Another practice that can assist teens with remembering lessons is the 3-2-1 Technique. This technique is meant to be used at the end of the lesson. First, teens are challenged to share three things they have learned during the lesson. Then, they share two things they found interesting about the biblical text. Finally, they share one question that they still have.[102] The benefit of this strategy is that teens must remember what they have learned and categorize what was most impactful for them.

Small group leaders can also assess learning throughout the lesson by utilizing the practice of Think-Pair-Share.[103] In this technique, small group leaders should strategically pause during the lesson and allow students to "think" about a question. Small group leaders can let guys pause and reflect silently, journal, draw, etc. during this moment. Usually, they will want to keep this pretty short unless it is a dynamic moment. Then, teens group in "pairs" to share their answers. By giving students a chance to think before they pair, the discussions are much more fruitful. Finally, the individual pairs come back together to the large group to "share" what they discussed with the larger group. This strategy gives the chance for everyone from the quietest introvert to the most outspoken to share what they are thinking in a setting that feels comfortable to them.

Enhance Care

Not only do we want to effectively teach guys in small groups, but we also want to effectively care for them. In an age where bullying and anxiety in guys continue to increase, leaders should create a safe place for teens to gather. Through a combination of care and active teaching, we create a better learning environment.

One of my favorite ways to enhance care in a small group is to start a group with "Highs, Lows, and Uh-Ohs." For this activity, small group leaders ask each teen to share one "high" point of the week, one "low" point of the week, and one "uh-oh" or mistake of the week. I am constantly surprised at how willing my guys are to share each time we do this. Sometimes, their responses are silly and fun and sometimes they are about serious things that have happened. Afterward, we can pray for one another. I have found that guys desire to share what is happening in their lives but don't always know how. This practice gives them the opportunity. We want to have fun with it, but we also want to protect the time so that guys feel safe to share.

We can also enhance care by creating a group covenant. The group covenant establishes how the small group will act. There are a few key aspects to a beneficial group covenant. First, we want to establish that there is safety in the group. We establish rules like not talking over someone who is sharing, listening to one another, and not sharing outside of the group. Second, we establish what we will do as leaders in the group. We establish that we will lead the group, will not tolerate bullying or pranks, will encourage each student, and will minister during times of need.

One final way youth workers can enhance care to guys is to equip our small group leaders to care for their students. First, youth ministers should equip leaders to share the gospel. Second, they should equip leaders with techniques to listen and show empathy. Finally, youth ministers should equip leaders with counseling tips for common issues in guys as well as learning when to refer them to a professional. Make sure your leaders know that if a child is harming himself or others, they immediately need to notify you and/or an authority. Train youth leaders how to assess whether a situation is beyond their training. At times it is necessary to bring the youth pastor, parents, or a professional into a situation with a student.

One Big Idea

This chapter has focused on utilizing simple active learning techniques. Periodically we as youth workers should study and use more complex techniques. Often, these techniques will not just be a teaching method in an individual lesson but a method to be employed for the whole semester or year. One alternative to try is creating a program or event from the learning. For example, when my guys and I wrote and led kids camp, that was a complex learning activity. This is not something that student ministries can do every year because of the amount of time and resources involved, but periodically creating a program or event leads to high motivation and buy-in from students, leaving them proud of their contributions.

If you choose to try a longer-duration period of active learning, I have a few suggestions. First, youth workers should be clear from the beginning stages about the nature of the project and the expectations. This not only builds excitement for the project but also ensures that the guys understand the responsibility they're undertaking. I have found that the more responsibility we give students, especially senior high guys, the more motivation they have and the more consistency they display.

Second, youth ministers should create scaffolding for success. Scaffolding allows for a project to be completed in stages. The chance of success greatly increases when we divide the final project into pieces to complete, allowing our guys to accomplish smaller tasks and receive feedback along the way to the final product. For the kids camp that my guys designed, we first created the theme, then we studied Scripture to write the study, and then we created the program elements. When the final project is broken down into steps, the task is more manageable, and the final product is much more successful.

Finally, youth ministers should use longer-term projects as opportunities to teach at a deeper level. Longer-term projects take more work, but they also give more time for growth, questions, course correction, and new ideas.[104]

A lot of times we think in ministry or small groups about a single lesson or program meeting. What if you planned something that you worked on all semester or year with your guys? Our students create presentations, papers, science fair projects, and projects in school. My own son in 7th grade is taking a year-long robotics course. Imagine if we challenged our guys to take what they were learning each week and create a journal or handbook for their own study, or created reproducible lesson plans they could use to disciple their teammates, or even developed a teaching series they could take on an international mission project!

12

Disciplemaking in Discipleship Groups

One Wednesday night a parent came up to me at church wanting to talk. Youth workers all know the feeling of conversations that start like this. It's like riding up the incline on a roller coaster not knowing what is waiting on the other side. Luckily, this conversation turned out to be a great one! This mom wanted to share how thankful she was that a senior guy was taking her seventh-grade guy to Sonic after school. Their plan was to read the Bible there together each week, then head to our church's midweek service together. This mom wanted me to know what an impact the senior was making on her son.

This senior guy was part of a group of three students I was discipling. We met weekly to read a chapter of the Bible, talk about spiritual disciplines, pray for one another, and find ways to serve. This was a closed group, meaning that we were not adding other members and these guys had agreed to meet weekly for the year. With these parameters I was able to go much deeper in the Bible with them, challenge them more specifically, build on prior learning because they were coming each week, and apply the lesson in specific ways that aligned with their giftings and places of leadership. My group of guys was just one of many similar groups meeting with our high school ministry.

When I began hearing other stories like this from parents, I knew that our youth ministry was thriving. I especially knew that we were thriving because I had no clue that this guy from my group was planning to spend time like this with a younger high schooler, and I had not told him to do so. I was excited because our student disciples were beginning to disciple others. This was evidence that our adult disciplers were becoming disciplemakers. These types of stories do not happen overnight. They come from years of intentional work in discipling teenagers.

Leaders use the term "discipleship groups" in many different ways. Some people call all their small groups discipleship groups. I am using the term "discipleship groups" as a different ministry element from small groups. When I use the term "small group," I am talking about groups of ten to fifteen students that intentionally mixes non-believers and believers. Students can join these groups at any time; thus, they are open groups. Small groups often will meet either after a large group teaching time or during a primary time in the church schedule, like a Sunday morning or midweek. When I use the term "discipleship group," I am talking about three to five students who are in a closed group for a fixed amount of time. These groups are for students who want to go deeper in their walks with God. Discipleship groups will often meet at a separate time than regular programming, like in the morning before school at a coffee shop.

Research Findings

Another question that I asked in my study on the faith maturity of teenage guys was, "How many adults would you say had an active role in your spiritual development during your teenage years?" I asked this to see if there are benefits for participating in multiple groups (such as small groups and discipleship groups) so that students have multiple adults pouring into their lives spiritually. The study showed that faith maturity scores were highest among the teens who had seven or more adults leading them spiritually. Teens with seven or more adults were categorized in the high faith maturity category, with the others in the moderate faith maturity.[105] We can take from this that ministries should find opportunities for multiple adults—ideally seven or more—to have an active role in a guy's spiritual walk.

My study's findings are similar to what others found in their research. Chap Clark writes, "Here's the bottom line: Every kid needs five adult fans. Any young person who shows any interest in Christ needs a minimum of five people of various ages who will say, 'I'm going to love that kid until they are fully walking as an adult member of this congregation.'"[106] Whether we're talking about five engaged adults or seven or more, the vision is for every student to have had at least five adults who have taken an active role in a guy's spiritual life. So, instead of focusing only on having one adult for every five students in a program or on a trip, youth workers should flip the script to work on creating an environment where every teen has the chance to connect with seven or more adults during their years in youth ministry.

Out of all the variables (e.g., number of adults, parent training events, Bible studies with just teenage guys, Bible studies with parents, sitting in worship as a family, etc.) in my study, the most powerful one affecting faith maturity was the number of adults who had an active role in a guy's spiritual development. We need to surround guys with a variety of caring adults. As previous chapters have shown, youth ministers start with equipping parents to disciple their children. Then, we expand the circle of adults to small group leaders who take an active role in each guy's spiritual development.

Discipleship groups are also important because of the depth of the relationship that can be established between teens and an adult leader. Because the discipleship group is small and closed, the leader can get to know each teen at a deeper level than what's possible in a larger, open small group. Ideally, each guy will have many adults in his life through various small group leaders, and at least one adult who knows him especially well through a discipleship group.

Small Changes ... Big Results

Strategically Build a Culture of Discipleship

We often speak of discipleship as a culture. As the saying goes, "Culture eats strategy for breakfast." By its nature, discipleship is organic and is most powerful when it takes place outside of our programs and systems. Still, we need to think strategically when it comes to discipleship, especially with teenage guys. Youth workers must create time and space for discipleship to happen consistently. Because discipleship is inherently a multiplication strategy, it will begin to occur organically over time.

Without a proactive strategy, we'll run into logistical issues that hinder discipleship. One of these logistical issues is students' lack of both transportation and time. Anyone who has tried to start a discipleship group of guys knows how difficult it is to find a time when everyone's busy schedules align so they can meet consistently—let alone when everyone has a ride to get there. That's not even taking into account our male leaders' busy work and family schedules. Then there are the logistics of safety and security. By nature, discipleship often occurs in a small group with deep connections, which can lead to child safety issues. Thus, discipleship leaders must find times and places to meet where they do not violate child safety procedures. Usually this means either a time when multiple groups are meeting in the same location or meeting in a public place, which can be difficult if meeting early in the morning before school. These issues alone can halt discipleship before it even gets off the ground.

In my previous church, I decided that for discipleship groups to have a chance, there needed to be a specific time to launch groups. I knew, and hoped, that these discipleship groups would eventually start meeting all throughout the week, but I also knew that the groups would always struggle if we didn't create an intentional time and structure for them to at least get started. Looking at my church's weekly schedule, I determined that Sunday nights were the best time to get discipleship groups going. We had open small groups on Sunday morning and a midweek service on Wednesday nights. On Sunday nights, we were not battling athletic or work schedules nearly as much as other times in the week. We also had plenty of space at our church facility to have multiple groups meeting simultaneously. Once they'd had their initial meetings and gotten into a rhythm of spending time together, some groups decided to meet at other times during the week.

For discipleship to begin to grow, a scheduled time must be consistent and protected. Nothing will kill a discipleship program quicker meeting inconsistently. Each fall, our groups started meeting in September and ran through Thanksgiving. After the New Year, they began again in February and continued through the spring, wrapping up in May. There were many times that I had to say no to other events during this time so that we could maintain consistency.

In addition to meeting consistently, we also built a bit more excitement about the groups by adding an element of fun. After our groups would finish, the guys in my group would play ultimate frisbee or team handball. These were games that every guy could participate in and allowed us to play together.

Build a Vision for Teen Disciplemaking

Not only do youth workers need to think strategically about time and space requirements, but also about how to build a vision for discipleship among their adult leaders. Before launching groups, I spent a semester reading a discipleship book with a few key leaders on our youth ministry team. We simply read the book and discussed it. So much of our vision for the groups came from what we read and talked about. Many of our best ideas came from the leaders, not me. Together, we began to decipher God's vision for our groups and how to get there from our current reality. The added benefit was that I had a group of adults who had taken ownership of the vision as it was being crafted. Whereas some events can be built quickly on the fly, discipleship takes time and wisdom—but the payoff is exponential.

Develop Adult Male Disciplemakers

As mentioned earlier in the book, a church may want to focus first on building strong discipleship groups for men in the church before creating discipleship groups for teenage guys. As the classic saying goes, "You can't lead someone to a place you are not already at." A disciplemaker by nature is spiritually more mature than the student he is discipling.

One way to develop adult male disciplemakers is for your church to offer adult discipleship groups, and look for potential youth ministry volunteers from these groups. As youth workers, we don't direct the adult discipleship process, but we can ask questions of those who do. At the church where I served, our staff spent time each week in our ministerial meeting updating the other staff members on how discipleship groups were going and if there was someone who could potentially serve or disciple others in our ministries.

Because there are many ways to do discipleship, youth workers should have discussions with the adult discipleship team to build community, encourage one another, and get new ideas. However, the adults are being discipled is most likely the way those adults will disciple teens. At my previous church, we decided that each lesson for every adult discipleship group needed to have a missional component, in keeping with the part of our mission statement that read, "Send them out." We picked a discipleship curriculum that included a weekly missional challenge. Thanks to our regular staff discussions, I knew this was what the adult discipleship team was doing, so I organized our youth ministry discipleship groups to also include a missional component each week.

Think Wisely About Group Formation

When creating a culture of disciplemaking, it's important to think wisely about group formation. For teenage guys, a group of three to five guys with a discipler is the sweet spot. If the group is formed with more than five guys, then the leader struggles to help the group members become comfortable being vulnerable. Leaders already struggle with getting guys to share meaningfully, and when the group is large, guys often shy away from sharing because they become worried about what the group will think. On the other hand, if the group is fewer than three, then the leader struggles with consistency. If one person can't make it one week, it significantly affects the group dynamics. Some guys may still share in a one-on-one session or two-on-one session, but many struggle with it and find it awkward, and they will benefit less from learning alongside one another.

In discipleship group formation, youth workers should also think wisely about the target audience for the program. When discipleship groups are being launched, adults often suggest recruiting guys who they see making bad decisions. My perspective is that small groups are better designed to reach these teens. These guys may also need individual counseling, either pastoral or professional, rather than discipleship. Discipleship groups aim at discipling students who are motivated to grow.

In college, we were taught by our campus ministry to look for F. A. T. students for discipleship. F. A. T. is an acronym that stands for faithful, attentive, and teachable.[107] In forming groups, leaders should look for guys who are already faithfully attending programs. These people tend to be intrinsically motivated, which means they'll likely attend discipleship groups regularly. As youth workers and small group leaders teach, they should also note which guys are actively listening. Finally, the students who thrive in discipleship groups are those who are teachable. Because discipleship occurs with a small group of guys and focuses on application, teens cannot hide. They will benefit the most if they are teachable. I have learned that it is more effective to begin with a smaller number of FAT guys and disciple them rather than launch a large program with all teens. These faithful, attentive, and teachable students will see great growth, and that will spread exponentially out to other groups over time.

Use Purposeful Curriculum

One of the big questions asked when building a discipleship program is what to use as curriculum. Before selecting curriculum, youth workers should first have a clear vision for what a mature Christian disciple looks like. It can be helpful to get a group of adult volunteers together and brainstorm what traits they would like to see in a discipled guy. I would like to see knowledge of the Word, a sure testimony, the ability to share the gospel, a compassionate and caring attitude for their neighbor, being a servant leader, being a discipler of others, having high moral character, missional living, and being an empathetic listener and a blessing to family and friends.

Once you have a clearer idea of what a discipled guys looks like, youth workers can then design a curriculum that will get them from where they currently are in their walks with God to being a disciple-maker. Every time we lead a discipleship lesson, we are simply seeking to help each teen take one small step toward the final picture.

It's important to think not just about the end goal, but the starting line. Youth workers should create a first steps plan for teens who are new in their faith. For those who are new in their faith or recently became members of our church, I typically would meet thirty minutes weekly with them for three or four weeks. We would cover topics such as the student's new life in Christ, the church, spiritual growth, and sharing the gospel with others. This onramp for the discipleship journey is an important part of discipleship.

There is also wisdom in starting every year of discipleship off with a foundational study of faith and discipleship. For a couple of weeks at the beginning of every discipleship year, I advise covering the gospel, how to grow in their walks with God (daily Bible reading plan, prayer, worship, small group involvement, etc.), and how to share their testimonies and the gospel with others. This also provides them with a basic plan to disciple their peers.

After the first couple of weeks focused on the foundations of faith, there are a variety of options groups can pursue. For some seasons, discipleship groups may want to spend time reading a book of the Bible, which gives leaders the chance to teach teens how to read and interpret Scripture. For many teenagers, this is a brand-new skill. In other seasons, discipleship groups may want to study a book together. I have seen teens struggle to sit down and read a book—it requires a lot more focus and time than scanning a social media post. One of my fears is that guys today scroll through their life like they scroll through social media. A book forces a student to slow down and think deeply about a subject. In some seasons, discipleship groups may want to study a resource specifically created for guys. While discipleship resources designed for girls far exceed those created for guys, there are some good options. Finally, discipleship groups may want to use discipleship resources with their small group curriculum. Many major publishers are now creating discipleship curriculum along with their small group curriculum.

I typically varied the curriculum that we studied from group to group, but I always make sure that the study we use brought our guys closer to the final picture of a discipled guy. While our curriculum changed in different seasons, I tried to keep a natural rhythm to group sessions. First, we would talk about our previous week and pray for one another. If I had assigned homework for the week, we would go over it. Second, we would talk about the current week's lesson. Sometimes this would involve reading a chapter in the Bible and sometimes it would involve discussing a chapter of a book we were reading. Third, we would spend time focusing on a spiritual discipline. Sometimes I would teach about a discipline and other times we would simply quote our memory verse of the week. Finally, we would end the session with a call to missional living. Often, this would include a charge to share with someone else what we had learned that week or encouragement to make a change in our own lives.

One Big Idea

Deploy College Students as Disciplemakers in Student Ministry

After I'd served for a decade at the same church, one of my major joys was seeing college students come back and serve as leaders in our ministry. They often invested back into our ministry by being leaders for the weekend retreats we held each January. When the college students were freshmen or sophomores, I would put them with seventh grade groups. Almost all of these college students would return as leaders the next year, and I would keep them with the same students. One benefit of this approach was that college students got to invest in the same teens over time. When the teenage guys were seniors, their college leaders were also finishing school or starting their career, marriage, etc. Not only were the college leaders celebrating the guys, but the guys were celebrating their college leaders by attending graduations, weddings, and the like. Spending time with these college students helped our junior high and high school guys get a picture of what it could look like to follow God in college and beyond.

13

Disciplemaking in Missional/Vocational Leadership

In *The Hobbit*, Tolkien describes a dragon, Smaug, who has amassed a treasure and hoards it away from everyone else.[108] The dragon is known throughout the land for stealing treasure and storing it in the mountain. He sits on his treasure and guards all he has stolen and hid.[109] His whole purpose for living is to keep what he has from everyone else. In our churches, we have men with incredible skills and giftings. Our churches are full of doctors, educators, lawyers, small business owners, CEOs, landscapers, fishermen, engineers, military leaders, contractors, writers, artists, historians, musicians, and the list goes on. Often in our ministries, our guys are only invited to connect with a handful of leaders. I wonder if we as youth workers are often more like Smaug the dragon than we intend to be, keeping our guys from a treasure trove of other adults who have so much to offer.

To use another *Hobbit* illustration, another character, Gandalf, sees the potential in a young hobbit. When all the dwarves are worried that this hobbit will be a hindrance to their mission, Gandalf grows large and proclaims that he has chosen Mr. Baggins for the journey. Gandalf realizes that Bilbo has more potential than Bilbo even realizes in himself. He also understands that Bilbo not only has a role to play in the journey, but also that the journey itself is important for Bilbo to grow into the hobbit that Gandalf knows he is.[110] Our guys today need someone in their life doing what Gandalf did for Bilbo. When I look at my own life, I would not be where I am today without my dad, pastors, professors, and mentors who noticed gifts that God had given me that I was just beginning to develop. I still vividly remember the moment one of my professors called me and asked if would teach a seminary class for him. That call was the first time I had been asked to teach and he told me he had full confidence in me. Here I am seventeen years later finishing my seventh year teaching full-time at the collegiate level. That call set me on a journey I would not have started if that professor did not see in me something I had not even considered yet.

A powerful moment occurs in a young boy's heart when an adult notices something in him—often something he doesn't yet see in himself—and begins to shine a light onto it as Gandalf does here with the young hobbit. We see echoes of this in the story of David being anointed king. The author of 1 Samuel writes,

> But the LORD said to Samuel, "Do not look at his appearance or his stature because I have rejected him. Humans do not see what the LORD sees, for humans see what is visible, but the LORD sees the heart." ... Then the LORD said, "Anoint him, for he is the one." So Samuel took the horn of oil and anointed him in the presence of his brothers, and the Spirit of the LORD came powerfully on David from that day forward.—1 Samuel 16:7, 12–13.

Our guys today desperately need to spend time with adults who recognize the work of God in their lives.

When I opened the door one Wednesday night for church, a group of tenth grade guys came in all wearing the same shirt, which bore the logo for their leader's lawn care business. I asked their leader why this was happening, and he said that they had all wanted to join his crew. He laughed at how many of them only lasted one day on the job, but how he was enjoying spending time with them outside of small group. That moment was a powerful picture to me of the opportunity that exists in connecting the skills, vision, purpose, and mission of adult men in our church to our young men.

Research Findings

In my research, I did not ask questions around the topics of vocational training/missional living, but since then I have spent some time reading in these areas. As mentioned in a previous chapter, often I have found that we miss taking opportunities to teach adolescents about the daily work of God in our lives. In his book *God at Work,* Gene Veith contends that through the rise of modernity and postmodernity, Christians have neglected the daily work of God. Veith asserts that in order to battle the claims of modernity, faith became focused on an individual's personal experience with God. The Sunday worship experience then became the primary, and sometimes only way, that Christians met with and experienced the work of God. The rest of the week, however, became the individual's own personal pursuit. While worship of God is a vital part of Christian faith, what became lost from the early church was the understanding that God was at work in our everyday lives. And that God expects us to serve Him and allow Him to work through us in our vocations and daily activities.[111]

When churches began focusing on experiential worship, they unintentionally forgot to also teach about God being at work in ordinary, everyday lives. Youth ministries have also focused on the experiences teens have at our programs. This is important, yet many have neglected teaching about God's work in human history and in our daily lives. Thus, teens meet with God on the weekends or Wednesday nights and then pursue their own dreams the rest of the week. This leads to students feeling connected to God in some ways but separating their current day-to-day activities and future vocations from God's calling.

In their studies of eighteen- to twenty-nine-year-olds who embody resilient discipleship, Kinnaman and Matlock found that "one of the highest reported levels of agreement resilient disciples show for *anything*" was that 94% of resilient disciples strongly agree on a desire to use their "unique talents and gifts to honor God." Nearly 90% also agreed that "God designs each person with a unique calling for their life." Kinnaman and Matlock also write, "the church desperately needs a richer theology of faith and faithfulness in life's complex callings, and we need to unite generations' seemingly disparate ways of understanding vocation."[112] Although Kinnaman and Matlock did not separate males and females in their study, my professor friends and I are seeing guys in particular struggling in their callings for the future. We are at a unique moment where we can help guys understand what God's calling in their life looks like, and how it affects many areas, including their vocation. Helping guys recognize the gifts God has given them is an important part of disciplemaking today.

When I was in high school, one of my neighbors had just started college. His first year did not go well. Then he discovered computer graphic animation and switched his major. I knew that he would excel in this with his love of movies and his creative mind. He quickly moved to the top of his major. Since then, he has worked on major motion pictures like *Avatar*. Once he discovered a major that matched his giftings and his passion, he soared. I think about that often when I am discipling guys. I had one guy who kept changing his major, and I never felt great about the majors he was choosing. I responded by giving him opportunities to serve and lead in our youth ministry in areas that would utilize the gifts that I saw in him, like teaching a small group. One day, he called to tell me that he was thinking about becoming a teacher. I immediately affirmed him in this and shared specific ways that I thought God had gifted him for this. As disciplemakers of guys, we sometimes get these moments to affirm God's calling and work in their lives.

Small Changes ... Big Results

Regularly Teach the Historical Work of God

One small change we can make to help guys see the work of God in their life is to teach the historical work of God in Scripture. The historical work of God is important because it shows the character and work of God and helps a guy to see how God is at work in his own life. When teaching Scripture, teachers would be wise to follow the psalmist's example in Psalm 78 of not speeding past the works of God in human history to get to individualist application of the text. Understanding the work of the Lord of history helps the current generation of guys to "shoot their arrows straight." The psalmist states in Psalm 78:9–11, "The Ephraimite archers turned back on the day of battle. They did not keep God's covenant and refused to live by his law. They forgot what he had done, the wondrous works he had shown them." In this case, the bows were ready, but the archers turned back from battle.

Along with connecting previous generations, youth workers and volunteer leaders should examine current liturgy and teaching to evaluate the extent of teaching of the historical work of God. In Psalm 78, the psalmist instructs that the works of the Lord of history should evoke wonder that leads to worship.[113] First, leaders should examine how much biblical history is taught in worship and teaching. Second, leaders should look at how much of the history of the church the church is teaching. I have benefited greatly from working with fellow professors who know the history of the church who have helped me to assess current events and issues through a historical framework, rather than just a crisis of the moment. Through these connections I've realized how little I did this for my students.

Plan Mission Trips

Although student leaders have to create experiential learning environments in small groups, mission trips are one hundred percent experiential learning. Mission trips are incredibly effective times of growth for teens. I have noticed this being particularly true for guys. Mission trips not only give guys opportunities to serve, but opportunities to learn. I love listening to guys share at the end of a mission trip all that God has taught them and how He has used them.

Even though mission trips are designed for all students, we can do a few things that will help those mission experiences to be more effective for guys specifically. First, youth workers should invite men to go on the trip with teenagers. Mission trips give a large quantity of time for teens to interact with men. Many great conversations can happen when guys are hanging out and debriefing what happened during the day.

Mission trips also give our guys a chance to observe adult men serving. Guys can learn a lot about manhood by observing men using their talents in mission work to serve others. One year, we were doing a backyard Bible club for children at an apartment complex. We had too many adults and students for the number of kids that showed up. One of our adult men who was a landscaper noticed that the playground needed some serious work. By the next day, he had gone to a hardware store and bought lumber to rebuild the edging of the playground and new mulch for underneath the equipment. When I came to the site the next day to see how it was going, I saw this man carrying one of the old, deteriorated pieces of lumber to the road with three teenage guys behind him helping. I snapped a picture with my phone because it reminded me of the importance of men using their skills to serve others and how teen guys will imitate them. These are the moments on mission trips that stick with us, when leaders are examples of service to God and others that teens can follow.

Paul states, "and you yourselves became imitators of us and of the Lord when, in spite of severe persecution, you welcomed the message with joy from the Holy Spirit. As a result, you became an example to all the believers in Macedonia and Achaia" (1 Thessalonians 1:6–7). This is still the formula for today. Adults model ministry to teens on mission trips, teens imitate the adults, and those we minister to then imitate the teens. That is disciplemaking!

Pre-trip preparation is a crucial step leading up to any mission trip. One thing to focus on during pre-trip preparation is the purpose of the mission and of the trip itself. Pre-trip preparation should include the study of God's Word, especially passages that will be used on the trip, and should teach specific skills to be used on the trip. I always love teaching how to prepare a spiritual testimony and often have had students accept Christ before the trip when they evaluated their personal testimony.

Pre-trip preparation also allows us to be intentional about utilizing all of our guys. I have found that guys are more likely to be engaged in the work if they feel prepared. Conversely, if they do not feel prepared, they will often sit back and disengage. We should start preparation by teaching them about the area where we are going. Then, we need to give them specific training for the work they will be doing. If it is yard work or construction, then they could collect their tools before the trip and maybe even do some local yard work or construction in advance. Although we typically think of using our guys for yardwork/construction sites, many guys will do well with children's activities, some guys will do well with sports ministries, and some guys will do well with relational ministry like with beachgoers, the homeless, or the elderly. If they might be leading activities for children's ministry, then the guys could practice teaching the lesson, leading the songs, and making the crafts. If they will be working with the homeless, then we could have great discussions on the causes of homelessness. If it is ministering to the elderly, then we can help our guys think about activities they can do while at the retirement home. One year, I had a group of students who worked with a church plant that was trying to reach the art district in Indianapolis. It was fun to see some of my creative guys really shine at this site. These guys would have been fine at a construction site, but they really exceled when they were involved with ministry activities that utilized their creative abilities.

Youth ministries should utilize guys in leadership positions on mission trips. This past week, I came across a missions brochure for college students. The brochure included a picture of a large group of college students serving in Boston. In that large group, there was only one guy. I wish that this picture was abnormal, but it accurately reflects what many missions agencies are seeing.

I took a group of students once to an international mission trip in Senegal, West Africa. On that trip, I had two recent high school graduate guys that I spent a lot of time with on the trip. One guy had been on summer mission trips with our student ministry every year since he was in middle school. The other guy had never been on a mission trip before. He took quite the leap to go on a two-week trip to a remote African village! As you can imagine, he hit a low a few days into the week. The student who had gone on many trips before began to share with the first-time mission trip participant that it is common to experience a hard day 3–4 days into the trip. He then shared that it is usually in those moments that God begins to really do something that only God can do. The years of taking the first student on mission trips, some locally and some throughout the states, built missional grit in his life. He was then prepared to equip this new student for missions. And I got to just sit back and watch him lead well.

Youth workers must make extra effort to recruit guys and call them to lead well. This will take intentional effort. I remember in high school thinking that my senior summer that I would skip the mission trip and work through the summer. One of our youth leaders intentionally sought me out and challenged me to finish my senior year well by going on the mission trip. I was so glad he did, and God used that summer to show me that I could use my summers in college to serve him. When I was in college, our campus minister asked me to go on a summer mission project with him and be a key leader on the team. That was a defining summer for me. Our guys need men who will call them toward service.

Provide Vocational Discipleship

Vocational discipleship provides a unique opportunity for connecting God's work in the present life of a guy. Whatever assignment God gives to our guys, it is an opportunity for them to connect God's work in their life, their service of others, and their service to God. Work is a practical way for guys to live on purpose for God and to serve others. One thing guys today struggle with is to think that only the most glorious or high-paying jobs are what matters. In God's kingdom, all work takes on significance when we are serving God and serving others.[114] Our teenage guys need to be challenged with this concept because they miss many opportunities to serve.

Adolescent males need a vision of being faithful and glorifying God in their present situations, such as schoolwork, part-time jobs, and extracurricular activities. As Kinnaman and Matlock write,

> This is one of the key opportunities presented to the twenty-first-century church: to infuse the vocational imaginations of this new generation with the purposes of God; to help them understand that God has made them *for* something; to learn from and emulate the integrated faith-work profile that resilient disciples display.[115]

The goal is not to prepare students to craft a better society in the future, but to serve others faithfully by allowing God to work through them right now. God is the One who gives us assignments and jobs. These are to be celebrated, no matter how glorious or how small the world might view them. In all these assignments, God is working through us to accomplish His purpose and will.[116] He might accomplish His will through ways we immediately recognize or it might be unnoticed as we serve others behind the scenes. Regardless, our guys need to be taught that everything God calls us to, vocationally and voluntarily, is an opportunity to join God in His work.

Many guys have been sold on the lie that vocation is something that they do to become something and to accumulate wealth and possessions. Veith reminds us that vocation is God at work in and through our teen guys.

Building a team of adult mentors in a job shadowing/internship program is one way of modeling for teens, and allowing them to practice, how God can work through each of us. The goal is to connect adolescent males with the older generation, not just to learn how to do a job, but also to witness how God can work through the teen in the profession. Youth workers serve in a unique position in that they have connections with many adults with a variety of vocational skills. We should find ways to leverage these opportunities and help our teens make connections with adults.

One Big Idea

Offer International Mission Trips

International mission trips offer some unique opportunities for our guys. Although all mission trips require mission prep time and allow our students to be in a new context, international mission trips require new types of prep work and provides our guys with a bigger picture of the work of God. International mission trips give us the opportunity to teach our teens about the culture that we will encounter. Guys especially can have tunnel vision on only the things they care about, like video games, their favorite YouTube channels, sports, weightlifting, etc. International mission trips raise their eyes up from their screens to the vastness of the world that God has created.

International mission trips require guys to put work into the trip. They have to get a passport, possibly get vaccines, study basic greetings and common phrases in another language, and prep for their ministry activities. We often try to make things so easy for our guys because we think that's how we'll attract them. Sometimes, though, they need to be challenged to put in some serious effort for a big task. Often, they will rise to the challenge and exceed it. One year, a high school guy who I was taking on an international trip to do a sport camp went to his soccer league and asked for guys to donate their old cleats to take on his trip because the previous year he'd seen guys from the community we were serving in the other country playing soccer barefoot. He ended up with three suitcases full of cleats, jerseys, and equipment to take on the trip with us! These trips give our guys an opportunity to rise above our low expectations and show the best they have to offer.

International mission trips also provide opportunities for our guys to meet other teenage guys in other parts of the world who are following God. There is just something powerful when a teen realizes that there is a spiritual connection with a guy he has never met. Despite their different backgrounds, they are brothers in Christ. It's good for our guys to hear the stories of how other teenagers are following God. On one trip, I almost couldn't get my guys in the taxi to make our flight back home to the U.S. because they were so engrossed in hearing from a local teenager about how he had been kicked out of his home when he accepted Christ, yet he continued to follow God. This teenager's story challenged them to live out their faith at home regardless of what obstacles they may encounter.

I encourage you to include senior adult men on these international trips. Older adults often have time to go on these longer trips than many younger men who are just starting their careers. When I was a young youth worker, I went on a vision trip to Africa with two older men. One was a retired international missionary who had served in Asia. The other man was seventy-plus and had been diagnosed with leukemia. That whole trip, I soaked up the wisdom from the two of them. I not only learned how to do missions in an international context but grew spiritually through our many conversations about God and life in general. On mission trips with older men, we get a massive quantity of time to build relationships and learn from one another. Our guys benefit not only from time spent with older generations of men on the trip itself, but also during pre-trip preparation. One of our senior adult men opened his home every week for dinner and training for our international mission trips. His wife spent all year on video calls with a language instructor learning the native language so that she could teach us the language. We could not have planted as many churches as we did in Africa if it was not for our senior adult encouragers!

Conclusion

A couple of months ago, I went to a wedding for one of the groups that was in the small group that threw the playdough ball through the window. Many of the guys from that group were there as well. We laughed at all of the stories that happened in that group. And we also marveled at how God is using each of those guys in the unique way that He has created them. I sat back and thought about all the lives they have already impacted for the kingdom and how many more they will impact through the rest of their lives.

The book of Nehemiah ends with a prayer that is repeated several times through Nehemiah: "Remember me, my God, with favor." Nehemiah asked that at the end of his life God would remember him and look with favor over all that he did. As we seek to disciple our guys, this is my prayer for us as well. "Remember us, our God, with favor." I pray that we would be faithful to the opportunity God has given us to disciple guys in this unique time. Let's rally to our guys by surrounding them with a caring group of adults. Let's teach these adults how to effectively lead guys groups through experiential and active learning. Let's create ministry programs that are designed to effectively disciple guys. And let's prepare our guys to be disciplemakers wherever God sends them. "Remember us, our God, with favor."

Appendix

Research Findings on Family Ministry Models and Male Faith Maturity

The data and research referenced in Part IV comes from my dissertation. The purpose of my dissertation was to analyze the differences between faith maturity of adolescent males and four family ministry models (both the model and individual ministry practices) for the purpose of proposing implications for the development of faith maturity in adolescent males. The first three of these family ministry models come from Timothy Paul Jones, who proposed that the three dominant models of family ministry are family-integrated, family-based, and family-equipping ministry.[117] The fourth family ministry model I included was a family-free model. The descriptive statements I used in the survey for these models are:

1. Family-free: My church had a youth ministry program that was led primarily by a youth minister and possibly a few adult leaders. The youth ministry program provided little or no opportunities for relationship building with adults outside the youth ministry.
2. Family-based: My church had a youth ministry program that was led primarily by a youth minister and adult leaders. The youth ministry program offered opportunities for me to build relationships with adults outside the youth ministry and encouraged my parents to participate in student events designed for parents and students.
3. Family-equipping: My church had a youth ministry program that was led by a youth minister and adult leaders, but also equipped and held my parents responsible to be my primary disciplemakers.

4. Family-integrated: My church expected my parents to be the primary persons who evangelized and discipled me. My church did not have an organized ministry specifically for youth because the generations did everything together.

Surveys were distributed to first-year freshmen male students at Charleston Southern University, Mississippi College, and the University of Mobile. The study was conducted during the fall of 2011 and involved 220 participants. To determine faith maturity, I used the Faith Maturity Scale survey instrument created by Benson, Donahue, and Erickson.[118] The Faith Maturity Scale utilizes a seven-point scale ranging from 1 (Never True) to 7 (Always True). The faith maturity score (mean) was determined for each student questionnaire by adding up the total score (with the reverse scoring questions) and dividing by total number of questions. A higher mean (up to 7) correlates with a more mature faith. I also developed a questionnaire on the family ministry model of the church the guys attended during their teenage years. I have included some of the research findings here.

Family Ministry Models and Faith Maturity

In my research, I asked participants to report the ministry model of the church they attended during their adolescent years. Instead of asking them to provide their own label, I created descriptive statements for each family ministry model, which were validated by an expert panel. The participants then chose which statement best fit the ministry they attended.

The responses of the participants are listed in table 1. Table 1 presents the family ministry model, the frequency of responses, and the percentage of responses. Figure 1 presents the frequency of the responses to the family ministry models.

Table 1: Frequency of Family Ministry Models

Model	Frequency	Percentage of Total Responses
No Family Ministry	14	6.4
Family-Free Ministry	50	22.7
Family-Based Ministry	118	53.6
Family-Equipping Ministry	32	14.5
Family-Integrated Ministry	6	2.7
Total	220	100.0

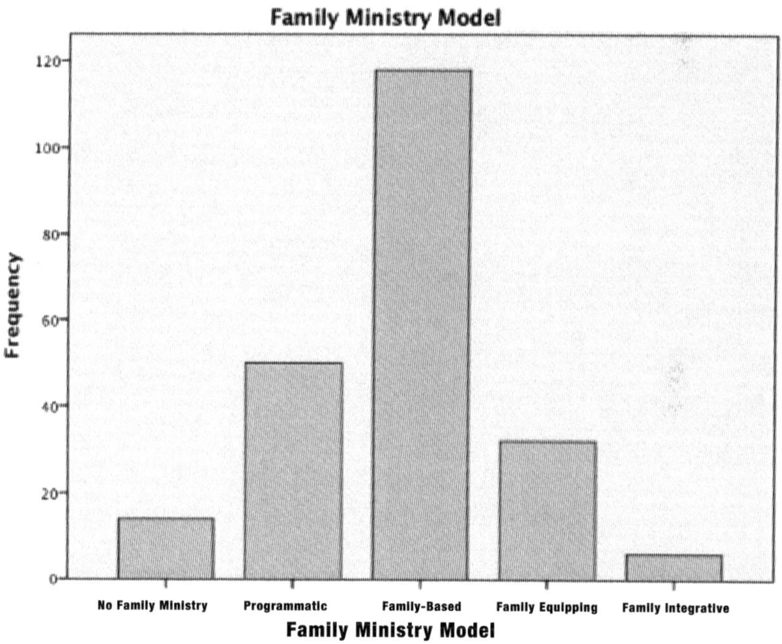

Fig. 1. Family Ministry Model Frequency Bar Chart

Of the 220 participants, over half (53.6%) described the church they attended during their adolescent years as using the family-based ministry model. The family-free ministry model made up 22.7% of the sample, and the family-equipping ministry model made up 14.5% of the sample. The no family ministry model (6.4%) and the family-integrated ministry model (2.7%) comprised the lowest percentage of respondents.

Table 2 summarizes the frequencies and Faith Maturity Score averages for each family ministry model and faith maturity score. All of the family ministry models fell into the moderate faith category on the faith maturity score, with the family-based ministry (4.94) and the family-equipping ministry (4.74) having the highest means. There was no significant difference found between the means of the different ministry models.

Table 2: Frequencies and Faith Maturity Score Means of Family Ministry Models

Models	Frequency	Faith Maturity Score Avg.
No Family Ministry	14	4.48
Family-Free Ministry	50	4.65
Family-Based Ministry	118	4.94
Family-Equipping Ministry	32	4.74
Family-Integrated Ministry	6	4.47
Total	220	4.80

The ministry models are similar in that all five ministry models have means that fall into the moderate faith category of the faith maturity scale. The moderate faith maturity category is between 3.00 and 4.99.

Significant Spiritual Talks at Special Moments

Because all five ministry models were similar in faith category, I began to study individual distinctives that are in some models and not in others to determine if any ministry practice (rather than model) makes a significant difference. One distinctive I studied was the impact of significant spiritual talks at special moments. The question stated, "Did your parents have significant spiritual talks with you during special moments in your life (thirteenth birthday, entering the youth group, getting your driver's license, first date, graduation, etc.)?" There were four possible responses: always, often, sometimes, and never.

Table 3 summarizes the frequencies and Faith Maturity Score averages for the four possible answers.

Table 3: Frequencies and Faith Maturity Score Means for Significant Spiritual Talks at Special Moments

Items	Frequency	Faith Maturity Score Avg.
Always	52	5.07
Often	65	4.79
Sometimes	63	4.72
Never	40	4.59
Total	220	4.80

The answer of always had the highest mean for faith maturity of 5.07. The answer of never had the lowest mean of 4.59. The study found a significant difference between the mean of always and never.

Family Worship Times

Another question I asked was: Did your parents lead family worship times or family Bible study at your house? Table 4 summarizes the frequencies and Faith Maturity Score averages for the four possible answers.

Table 4: Frequencies and Faith Maturity Score Means for Family Worship Times

Items	Frequency	Faith Maturity Score Avg.
Always	21	4.85
Often	28	5.02
Sometimes	70	4.79
Never	101	4.74
Total	220	4.80

Over 75% of the participants responded that their families never or just sometimes had family worship times or Bible study at their homes. The high percentage is not surprising. Timothy Paul Jones stated that the second factor in the low practice of parents discipling their children was that parents were too busy to make spiritual development of their children a priority. Jones also found that 35% of parents have not offered family devotional or worship time in their homes in the last two months.[119] Almost half of the participants (45.9%) responded that their families never had family worship times or Bible study at their homes. This is an area where youth ministries can equip parents.

Parent Training Events

This led to asking: To the best of your knowledge, did your parents attend parent training events offered by the church you attended during your teenage years? Table 5 summarizes the frequencies and Faith Maturity Score averages for the four possible answers.

Table 5: Frequencies and Faith Maturity Score Means for Frequency of Parent Training Events

Items	Frequency	Faith Maturity Score Avg.
Always	7	5.04
Often	19	4.99
Sometimes	79	4.87
Never	115	4.71
Total	220	4.80

The high frequency of responses of never is somewhat surprising given the number of participants who responded that the church they attended during their teenage years was family-based. One possible explanation could be that teenagers are not aware of the training opportunities that are offered to parents by the church they attend. A more likely explanation is that churches may be family-based in some ways but are doing a poor job of equipping parents. Timothy Paul Jones found that one of the two main factors in the low practice of discipling children was that the church was not properly training parents to disciple their children.[120]

Father Involvement in Spiritual Growth

I also asked: Did your father take an active role in your spiritual growth during your teenage years? Table 6 summarizes the frequencies and Faith Maturity Score averages for the four possible answers.

Table 6: Frequencies and Faith Maturity Score Means for Father Involvement in Spiritual Growth

Items	Frequency	Faith Maturity Score Avg.
Always	61	4.97
Often	35	4.65
Sometimes	51	4.84
Never	73	4.71
Total	220	4.80

There was almost an equal frequency of the "always" and "never" responses. Over 40% (43.6%) of participants had fathers who always or often took an active role in the adolescent male's spiritual growth during his teenage years. The finding of no significant difference in faith maturity is surprising. Andrew Clyde Parker found a significant correlation between father nurturance and spiritual development among adolescents, with 40% of spiritual development attributed to father nurturance.[121] Although encouraging that over 40% of fathers took an active role in their sons' spiritual growth, there are still many fathers who do not. Those who do have a great opportunity to disciple other fathers.

Bible Study Groups With Teenage Guys

Another question I posed in my study was about the impact of Bible study groups for teenage guys and how that affect faith development. Table 7 summarizes the frequencies and Faith Maturity Score averages for the four possible answers.

Table 7: Frequencies and Faith Maturity Score Means for Bible Study Groups With Teenage Guys

Items	Frequency	Faith Maturity Score Avg.
Always	32	5.22
Often	40	4.89
Sometimes	61	4.90
Never	87	4.54
Total	220	4.80

The faith maturity score means increased the more that a student spent in Bible study groups with teenage guys. The lowest average score was those who never attended Bible study groups with teenage guys. There appears to be some spiritual benefit for teenage guys to be in a Bible study with other teen guys.

Bible Study Groups With Parents

I also tested to see how many students attended Bible studies with their parents and if these family Bible studies made a significant difference on their faith maturity. Table 8 summarizes the frequencies and Faith Maturity Score averages for the four possible answers.

Table 8: Frequencies and Faith Maturity Score Means for Attending Bible Studies With Their Parents

Items	Frequency	Faith Maturity Score Avg.
Always	23	5.28
Often	22	4.67
Sometimes	48	4.82
Never	127	4.73
Total	220	4.80

Over half of the participants (57.7%) never attended the same weekly Bible study groups with their parents. The responses in this category included the highest number of "never" answers out of all of the questions. But those who always had Bible study groups with their parents (10.5%) showed significantly higher Faith Maturity Score. The mean was similar to those who always attended Bible studies with teenage guys.

Number of Adults With Significant Role in Spiritual Development

Another question that I asked in my study was, "How many adults would you say had an active role in your spiritual development during your teenage years?" There were six possible answers: 0, 1–2, 3–4, 5–6, 7–9, and 10+. Table 9 summarizes the frequencies and Faith Maturity Score averages for the four possible answers.

Table 9: Frequencies and Faith Maturity Score Means for Number of Adults who had a Significant Role in Spiritual Development

Models	Frequency	Faith Maturity Score Avg.
0	5	3.75
1–2	32	4.52
3–4	69	4.75
5–6	52	4.78
7–9	17	5.16
10+	45	5.09
Total	220	4.80

Guys who had 7+ adults take an active role in their spiritual development during their teenage years had the highest Faith Maturity Scores. Students with 7–9 adults and 10+ adults were categorized in as having high faith maturity, with the others were categorized as having moderate faith maturity.[122] A significant difference occurred between the answer of 0 adults and 1–2 adults. A significant difference also occurred between the answers of 1–2 adults and the answers of 7–9 adults and 10+ adults.

Best Predictor of Faith Maturity

Next, a stepwise multiple regression was conducted to evaluate which distinctive questions best predicted faith maturity. A stepwise multiple regression is used when there are multiple variables to find out which variables are the strongest predictors of the outcome, in this case Faith Maturity. When the stepwise multiple regression equation is run, it will include the questions that predict the outcome. The stepwise regression equation for the standardized variables is used so that the variable with the most powerful coefficient can be determined.

The stepwise regression equation for the variables used in my survey is:

Faith Maturity Score = 3.49 + .128 *(Bible Study Groups of Teenage Guys)* + .116 *(Number of Adults who Take an Active Role)* + .103 *(Bible Study Groups with Adolescents and Parents)* + *.127 (Activities and Worship for Youth Separate from Adults).*

The stepwise regression equation for the standardized variables is:

$$Z_{\text{Faith Maturity Score}} = .190\ Z_{\text{Bible Study Groups of Teenage Guys}} + .225\ Z_{\text{Number of Adults who Take an Active Role}} + .143\ Z_{\text{Bible Study Groups with Adolescents and Parents}} + .148\ Z_{\text{Activities and Worship for Youth Separate from Adults}}$$

The stepwise regression equation found that the factors that best predicted faith maturity in adolescent guys consisted of Bible study groups with only teenage guys, the number of adults who had an active role in the spiritual development of an adolescent male, weekly Bible study groups with parents and adolescent males, and church programming that included activities and worship for youth separate from adults. The most powerful coefficient in the equation was the number of adults who had an active role in the spiritual development of an adolescent male.

Endnotes

[1] Andrew Yang, "Opinion: The Data Are clear: The Boys Are Not All Right," *The Washington Post*, February 8, 2022, accessed 21 March 2022, https://www.washingtonpost.com/opinions/2022/02/08/andrew-yang-boys-are-not-all-right/.

[2] Michael Gurian and Kathy Stevens, *The Minds of Boys* (San Francisco: Jossey-Bass, 2005), 22.

[3] Michael Kimmel, *Guyland: The Perilous World Where Boys Become Men* (New York: HarperCollins, 2008), 3–4.

[4] Leonard Sax, *Boys Adrift* (New York: Basic Books, 2007), 7.

[5] Greg Stier, "The Gospel Advancing View of Youth Ministry" in *Youth Ministry in the 21st Century: Five Views*, Chap Clark, ed. (Grand Rapids: Baker Academic, 2015), 4.

[6] Timothy Keller, *Counterfeit Gods* (New York: Penguin Books, 2009), xix.

[7] Douglas Belkin, "A Generation of American Men Give Up on College: 'I Just Feel Lost,'" *The Wall Street Journal*, September 6, 2021, accessed 3 Oct 2022, https://www.wsj.com/articles/college-university-fall-higher-education-men-women-enrollment-admissions-back-to-school-11630948233.

[8] L. S. Vygotsky, *Educational Psychology*, trans. Robert Silverman (Boca Raton, FL: St. Lucie Press, 1997), 33.

[9] Catherine Twomey Fosnot and Randall Stewart Perry, "Constructivism: A Psychological Theory of Learning," in *Constructivism: Theory, Perspectives, and Practice*, ed. Catherine Twomey Fosnot, 2d ed. (New York: Teacher College Press, 2005), 22.

[10] L. S. Vygotsky, *Mind in Society*, ed. Michael Cole, Vera John-Steiner, Sylvia Scribner, and Ellen Souberman (Cambridge: Harvard University Press, 1978), 86.

[11] David Walsh, *Why Do They Act That Way? A Survival Guide to the Adolescent Brain for You and Your Teen* (New York: Free Press, 2004), 32–36.

[12] Joe S. McIlhaney Jr. and Freda McKissic Bush, *Hooked: New Science on How Casual Sex Is Affecting Our Children* (Chicago: Northfield Publishing, 2008), 50.

[13] Amanda Onion, "Scientists Find Sex Differences in Brain," ABC News, January 19, 2005, accessed January 27, 2011, http://abcnews.go.com/Technology/Health/story?id=424260&page=1.

[14] R. K. Lenroot and J. N. Giedd, "Brain Development in Children and Adolescents: Insights from Anatomical Magnetic Resonance Imaging," *Neuroscience and Biobehavioral Reviews* 30 (2006): 718–729.

[15] R. K. Lenroot and J. N. Giedd, "Sex Differences in the Adolescent Brain," *Brain and Cognition* 72, no. 1 (February 2010): 46–55.

[16] Gurian and Stevens, *The Minds of Boys*, 45.

[17] Gurian and Stevens, *The Minds of Boys*, 49.

[18] Gurian and Stevens, *The Minds of Boys*, 48-50.

[19] Gurian and Stevens, *The Minds of Boys*, 48-51.

[20] Gurian, *A Fine Young Man* (New York: Jeremy P. Tarcher/Putnam, 1998), 38.

[21] Michael Gurian, *The Good Son* (New York: Jeremy P. Tarcher/Putnam, 2000), 29.
[22] Gurian and Stevens, *The Minds of Boys*, 43–45.
[23] Gurian, *The Good Son*, 36.
[24] Gurian, *A Fine Young Man*, 181–184.
[25] Sax, *Boys Adrift*, 28-30.
[26] Warren Farrell and John Gray, *The Boy Crisis* (Dallas: BenBella Books, Inc., 2018), 9.
[27] Farrell and Gray, 105.
[28] Kimmel, 42.
[29] Peter L. Benson, Michael J. Donahue, and Joseph A. Erickson, "The Faith Maturity Scale: Conceptualization, Measurement, and Empirical Validation," *Research in the Social Scientific Study of Religion* 5 (1993): 3–4.
[30] James Fowler, "The Vocation of Faith Development Theory," in *Stages of Faith and Religious Development: Implications for Church, Education, and Society*, ed. Karl Ernst Nipkow, Friedrich Schweitzer, and James Fowler (New York: Crossroad, 1991), 25.
[31] Christian Smith and Melinda Lundquist Denton, *Soul Searching: The Religious and Spiritual Lives of American Teenagers* (New York: Oxford University Press, 2005), 39.
[32] Smith and Denton, 34.
[33] Smith and Denton, 57.
[34] Peter L. Benson and Carolyn H. Eklin, "Effective Christian Education: A National Study of Protestant Congregations," *Search Institute*, March 1990, 39.
[35] Smith and Denton, 277, 279.
[36] Sax, *Boys Adrift*, 170.
[37] Michael Gurian, *The Wonder of Boys* (New York: Jeremy P. Tarcher/Penguin, 2006), 58–61.
[38] Chap Clark, "The Adoption View of Youth Ministry," *Youth Ministry in the 21st Century: Five Views*, edited by Chap Clark (Grand Rapids: Baker Academic, 2015), 83.
[39] Richard A. Hardel and Merton P. Strommen, *Passing on the Faith: A Radical New Model for Youth and Family Ministry* (Winona, MN: St. Mary's Press, 2000), 66.
[40] Gurian and Stevens, *The Minds of Boys*, 34–35.
[41] Richard Ross, *Student Ministry and the Supremacy of Christ* (Bloomington, IN: CrossBooks, 2009), 39.
[42] Ron Hunter, "The D6 View of Youth Ministry," *Youth Ministry in the 21st Century: Five Views*, edited by Chap Clark (Grand Rapids: Baker Academic, 2015), 148–149.
[43] Sax, *Boys Adrift*, 169.
[44] Gurian and Stevens, *The Minds of Boys*, 280–181.
[45] David Elkind, *All Grown Up and No Place to Go: Teenagers in Crisis*, revised edition (New York: Da Capo Press, 1998), 94.

Endnotes

[46] "Data and Statistics on Children's Mental Health," Centers for Disease Control and Prevention, accessed March 17, 2022, https://www.cdc.gov/childrensmentalhealth/data.html#ref.

[47] Farrell and Gray, 15.

[48] "Suicide," National Institute of Mental Health, accessed March 17, 2022, https://www.nimh.nih.gov/health/statistics/suicide#part_2557.

[49] Gurian, *A Fine Young Man*, 111.

[50] Smith Denton, 162–163.

[51] Derek Kidner, *Psalms 73-150: A Commentary on Books III-V of the Psalms* (Downers Grove: Inter-varsity Press, 1973), 280.

[52] Gene Edward Veith, Jr. *God at Work: Your Christian Vocation in All of Life* (Wheaton: Crossway, 2002), 59.

[53] Fernando Arzola, "The Ecclesial View of Youth Ministry" in *Youth Ministry in the 21st Century: Five Views*, edited by Chap Clark (Grand Rapids: Baker Academic, 2015), 116–117.

[54] *CSB Study Bible* (Nashville: Holman Bible Publishers, 2017), 844.

[55] James Luther Mays, *Psalms*, Interpretation: A Bible Commentary for Teaching and Preaching, edited by James Luther Mays (Louisville: John Knox Press, 1994), 255.

[56] John Goldingay, *Psalms,* vol. 2 Psalms 42–89, *Baker Commentary on the Old Testament Wisdom and Psalms*, edited by Tremper Longman III (Grand Rapids: Baker Academic, 2007), 485.

[57] Mays, 256.

[58] Mays, 255.

[59] Goldingay, 480.

[60] Paul David Tripp, *Age of Opportunity: A Biblical Guide to Parenting Teens* (Phillipsburg, NJ: P&R Publishing, 1997), 42.

[61] Michael S. Lawson, "Old Testament Teachings on the Family," *A Theology for Family Ministries*, ed. Michael Anthony and Michelle Anthony (Nashville: B&H Publishing Group, 2011), 76–77.

[62] Robert L. Plummer, "Bring Them Up in the Discipline and Instruction of the Lord: Family Discipleship among the First Christians," *Trained in the Fear of God: Family Ministry in Theological, Historical, and Practical Perspective*, ed. Randy Stinson and Timothy Paul Jones (Grand Rapids: Kregel Publications, 2011), 54–55.

[63] Mark Senter III, "Axioms in Youth Ministry," *The Complete Book of Youth Ministry*, ed. Warren S. Benson and Mark H. Senter III (Chicago: Moody Press, 1987), 207.

[64] Tripp, *Age of Opportunity*, 59.

[65] Smith and Denton, 57.

[66] Timothy Paul Jones, *Family Ministry Field Guide* (Indianapolis: Wesleyan Publishing House, 2011), 99, 215.

[67] Jones, *Family Ministry Field Guide,* 29–30.

[68] Jones, *Family Ministry Field Guide*, 101.

[69] Mark Oestreicher and Scott Rubin, *Middle School Ministry: A Comprehensive Guide to Working With Early Adolescents* (El Cajon, CA: Youth Specialties, 2009), 11.
[70] Chap Clark, "The Changing Face of Adolescence: A Theological View of Human Development" *Starting Right: Thinking Theologically about Youth Ministry*, edited by Kenda Creasy Dean, Chap Clark, and Dave Rahn (El Cajon, CA: Youth Specialties Academic, 2001), 50.
[71] Clark, *Starting Right*, 54.
[72] Nancy J. Cobb, *Adolescence: Continuity, Change and Diversity*, 5th ed. (Boston: McGraw Hill, 2004), 107–109.
[73] Malcolm Gladwell, *Outliers: The Story of Success* (New York: Little, Brown and Company, 2008), 30–31.
[74] Walt Mueller, *The Space Between: A Parent's Guide to Teenage Development* (Youth Specialties: El Cajon, 2009), 42.
[75] Oestreicher and Rubin, 38.
[76] Reggie Joiner and Kristen Ivy, *It's Just a Phase So Don't Miss It* (Orange Books, 2015), 93–94.
[77] "Olympic Gold Medalist Red Gerard Recalls 'Hectic' Morning Before Big Win," February 14, 2018, accessed February 18, 2022, https://abcnews.go.com/Entertainment/olympic-gold-medalist-red-gerard-recalls-hectic-morning/story?id=53070408.
[78] Joiner and Ivy, 95.
[79] David Elkind, *The Hurried Child: Growing Up Too Fast Too Soon* (Reading: Addison-Wesley Publishing Company, 1982), 116.
[80] Elkind, *All Grown Up and No Place to Go: Teenagers in Crisis* (1984), 40–41.
[81] Richard M. Lerner, *Adolescence: Development, Diversity, Context, and Application* (Upper Saddle River, NJ: Prentice Hall), 102.
[82] F. Philip Rice and Kim Gale Dolgin, *The Adolescent: Development, Relationships, and Culture* (Boston: Pearson, 2008), 125.
[83] Keller, xix.
[84] James M. Lang, *Small Teaching* (San Francisco: Jossey-Bass, 2016), 10.
[85] Benson, Donahue, and Erickson, 1.
[86] Peter L. Benson and Carolyn H. Eklin, "Effective Christian Education: A National Study of Protestant Congregations," *Search Institute*, March 1990, 10.
[87] Benson and Elkin, 10.
[88] Benson, Donahue, and Erickson, 1.
[89] Timothy Paul Jones, ed., *Perspectives on Family Ministry: 3 Views* (Nashville: Broadman & Holman Academic, 2009), 42–44.
[90] Paul David Tripp, *Parenting* (Wheaton: Crossway, 2016), 87.
[91] Jones, *Family Ministry Field Guide*, 29–30, 101.
[92] Jones, *Family Ministry Field Guide*, 101.
[93] Tripp, *Parenting*, 87.

Endnotes

[94] Tripp, *Parenting*, 92.
[95] Smith and Denton, 57.
[96] Tripp, *Parenting*, 30.
[97] Tripp, *Parenting*, 97.
[98] Jim Herrington, Mike Bonem, and James H. Furr, *Leading Congregational Change* (San Francisco: Jossey-Bass, 2000), 107.
[99] Lang, 18.
[100] Lang, 24.
[101] Texas A&M Academic Success Center, "Reading Strategies: The KWL Method," accessed March 5, 2022, https://asc.tamu.edu/study-learning-handouts/reading-strategies-the-kwl-method.
[102] The Teacher Toolkit, "3–2–1," accessed March 5, 2022, http://www.theteachertoolkit.com/index.php/tool/3-2-1.
[103] Reading Rockets, "Think-Pair-Share," accessed March 5, 2022, https://www.readingrockets.org/strategies/think-pair-share.
[104] Lang, 95–96.
[105] Benson and Eklin, 12.
[106] Chap Clark, "In Spite of How They Act … Teenagers Don't Want to Be Left Alone," *Decision Magazine*, August 17, 2004, accessed March 5, 2022, https://decisionmagazine.com/in-spite-of-how-they-act/.
[107] Colin Marshall and Tony Payne, *The Vine Project* (Youngstown, OH: Matthias Media, 2016), 22.
[108] J.R.R. Tolkien, *The Hobbit: Or There and Back Again*, note on the text edition, (Boston: Houghton Mifflin Company, 1995), 18.
[109] Tolkien, 27.
[110] Tolkien, 23.
[111] Gene Edward Veith, Jr. *God at Work: Your Christian Vocation in All of Life* (Wheaton: Crossway, 2002), 28.
[112] David Kinnaman and Mark Matlock, *Faith for Exiles: 5 Ways for a New Generation to Follow Jesus in Digital Babylon* (Grand Rapids: Baker Books, 2019), 146–147.
[113] Goldingay, 480.
[114] Veith, 59.
[115] Kinnaman and Matlock, 151.
[116] Veith, 29–30.
[117] Jones, ed., *Perspectives on Family Ministry*, 42–44.
[118] Benson, Donahue, and Erickson, 1.
[119] Jones, *Family Ministry Field Guide*, 29–30, 101.
[120] Jones, *Family Ministry Field Guide*, 101.
[121] Andrew Clyde Parker, "An Analysis of the Relationship Between Adolescent Spiritual Development and Father Involvement" (Ph.D. diss., The Southern Baptist Theological Seminary, 2010), 114.
[122] Benson and Eklin, 12.